To Alex, with love

ACKNOWLEDGMENTS

Above all my thanks go to Alex – for his support, encouragement and constructive criticism, and for putting up with me while museums became my obsession. I am indebted to Christina Ballinger, not only for generously sharing her knowledge of the museum world and the issues which concern it, but also for her infectious enthusiasm. Isabelle van Lennep's timely provision of essential research materials was much appreciated, and I am grateful to Maurice Davies for allowing me to pick his brains about London's museums. Thanks also to Ally Ireson for her editorial work, and to Andrew Kershman and Susi Koch for their help during the preparation of the book and for providing the photos and maps. Finally, my heartfelt thanks to all the curators and museum staff who (as if they didn't have enough to worry about already) let me look around their museums, sent me information, answered my questions and without whose assistance and co-operation this book would not have been possible.

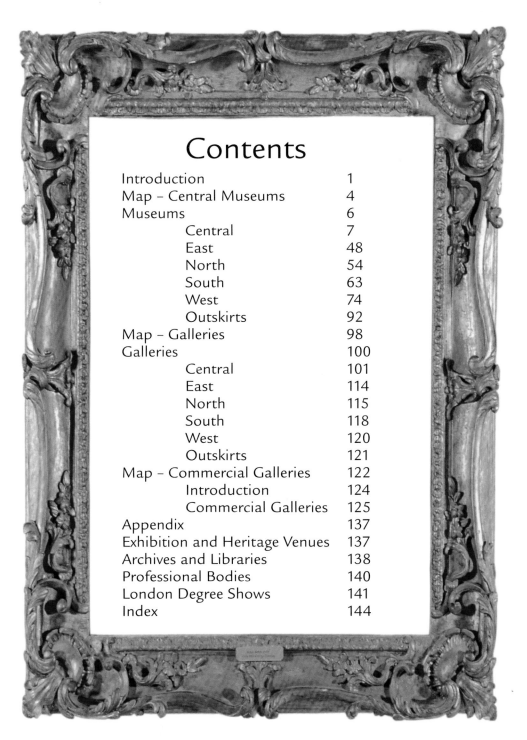

Contents

ABOUT THE AUTHOR

Abigail Willis studied history of art at Reading University and has worked as a picture researcher at the Courtauld Institute of Art and for Waddington Galleries. She has written for 'The Evening Standard' and 'The Church Times', and is a contributor to 'Galleries and Studio Pottery' magazine. Her previous books include 'Bloomsbury Ceramics', published by Cecil Woolf and 'The Parables of Jesus, and their place in Christian Art', published by Penguin Studio, New York. 'Museums and Galleries of London' is her first guide book.

She lives in north London with her husband, film maker Alexander Ballinger.

INTRODUCTION

L ondon's museumscape is as diverse and individual as the city itself. From world famous tourist magnets like the British Museum to smaller museums serving local communities to quirky independents, the capital's museums and galleries offer terrific choice for urban explorers. Whether you're interested in dinosaurs or dentistry, freemasonry or firefighting, Old Masters or Young British Artists chances are there's a museum covering the subject. And as well as being a kind of 3-D encyclopedia, London's museums and galleries (whatever their specialisation) provide an unrivalled insight into the history of the city, and the achievements, tastes and lives of its inhabitants.

As the century gallops to a close, London's museum scene goes from strength to strength. Shaking off their stuffy, dusty image of old, national institutions such as the Tate Gallery, the Natural History Museum and the Science Museum have reinvented themselves over the past decade to become crowd-pulling leisure destinations. Stimulating exhibitions, dynamic education departments organising a spectrum of events, enticing on site shops and improved cafés have all been by-products of this renaissance. More good news for visitors is that non-nationals have had to pull their socks up too – as the abundance of 'customer charters' in museum hallways suggests.

The convergence of the Millennium and the National Lottery (with its handouts for 'good causes') has galvanised the museums sector afresh. New building projects have been mushrooming over the capital in readiness for the year 2000 – the British Museum, the Wallace Collection, the Geffrye Museum and the National Portrait Gallery to name but a few – so that come the new century, museum-goers will have even more to enjoy.

So, there's no doubt that it's an exciting time for London's museums and galleries and, with more of them in the capital than ever before, this guide aims to help visitors and residents alike to get the most out of the city's remarkable cultural resources. The book is divided into four sections: Museums (which includes historic houses), Galleries (detailing London's public art venues), Commercial Galleries (which presents a cross-section of London's world class 'selling galleries', and includes a separate introduction), and an Appendix (listing various art venues, archives, useful addresses and end of year degree shows). Entries are arranged by area with maps to help you find your way around but, before you set out on your voyage of discovery, let me pass on a few hard-won tips gleaned during the months spent researching this book.

For a frustration-free visit, it's always worth telephoning the museum (particularly the smaller ones) you're planning to visit before setting out. There's nothing more aggravating than traipsing across town to find a place closed or to discover the work of art you specifically wanted to see is away on a six-month tour of the world. Millennial building works, staff shortages, acts of God, the curator's punctured bicycle tyre and bank holidays are all likely to affect opening times – so RING FIRST.

Thanks to legislation, disabled access at museums has improved over the past 15 years or so, although its provision varies enormously from place to place. Although I have tried to include a general indication of which public venues have disabled access it's advisable to either ring the venue for more detailed information or contact the very helpful staff at ARTSLINE on 0171 388 2227, the free information service on the arts in Greater London for people with disabilities.

Museum going can be an expensive business but there's no need to pay over the odds. The White Card offers unlimited access to 15 of London's top museums and galleries and is valid for either 3 days or 7 days (the latter being the more cost effective option). Costing from £15 for the 3 day version, this saver pass is available from each participating venue, and London Transport Information Centres, or by telephoning First Call (0171 420 0000) or Ticketmaster (0171 344 4444).

The 'Big Three' at South Kensington offer their own annual season ticket but bear in mind that several admission-charging museums have free entry one day a week or – for hit and run culture vultures – after certain times of the day. A number of museums also run Friend's schemes which offer free entry along with perks like priority booking and exclusive events.

Museum going can be hard on the stomach too and, although in general standards are improving, in-house cafés can be bland, pricey and over-crowded. Packed lunches are one solution, particularly for families, and many museums provide pleasant picnics areas. Alternatively jump ship for an hour or two (make sure your ticket has re-entry) to explore some of the local caffs - they're invariably better value and more atmospheric. I've included a few of my favourites here.

And finally, don't forget that (apart from this guide) the best companion a museum-goer can have is a comfortable pair of shoes.

I hope you will enjoy exploring London's museums and galleries as much as I have.

Abigail Willis, London, June 1998

MAP MUSEUMS - CENTRAL

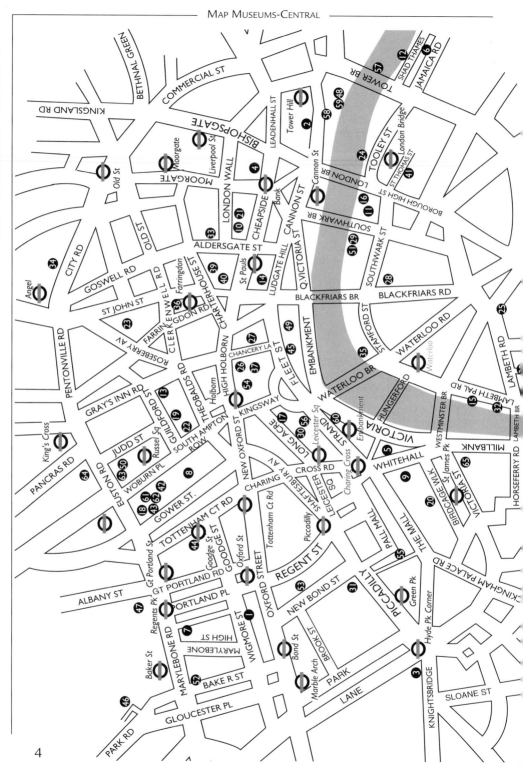

MAP MUSEUMS - CENTRAL

MUSEUMS

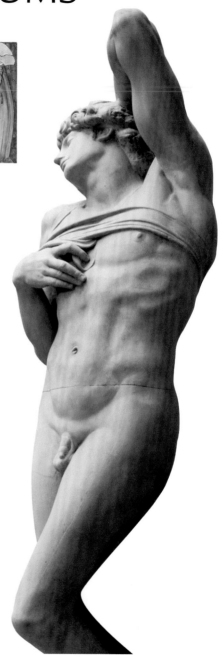

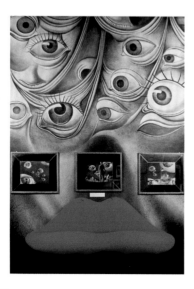

CENTRAL

Alfred Dunhill Collection

- 🖵 *30 Duke Street, W1*
- 🕐 *0171 838 8000 (curator: Howard Smith)*
- 🚌 *Transport: Piccadilly Circus LU, Green Park LU*
- 🕐 *Mon-Fri 9.30-18.00, Sat 10.00-18.00*
- ♨ *Admission free*
- ♿ *Wheelchair access*
- 🛍 *Shop*

Elegant Art Deco style surroundings, deep pile carpets, palms and softly piped jazz make this one of the plushest museums in town. Motoring and smoking seem to be the main focus of the displays with many items dating from the days when either one or both pursuits conferred instant glamour on the participant. Auto enthusiasts will just love the voluminous leather driving coats, motorist's 'windshield' pipe and the 'Bobby Finders' which promise to 'spot a policemen at half a mile'. Other luxury knick-knacks include jewel-like lacquered cigarette lighters from the 1920's, a portable cocktail cabinet and a handbag with its own interior light. For those who appreciate the finer things in life.

All Hallows by the Tower Undercroft

- 🖵 *Byward Street, EC3*
- 🕐 *0171 481 2928*
- 🚌 *Transport: Tower Hill LU*
- 🕐 *Mon-Sat 11.00-16.00*
- ♨ *Admission £2.50 (audio guide)*
- 🛍 *Shop*

This tranquil church is worlds away from the teeming tourist trap that is Tower Hill. The audio tour of the undercroft museum is compulsory but provides useful commentary on the exhibits, which range from archaeological finds and church plate to a tessellated Roman floor and rare Anglo-Saxon stone crosses. Founded in AD675, All Hallows is one of London's most historic churches: Samuel Pepys watched the Great Fire from its tower and William Penn, the founder of Pennsylvania, was baptised here (the beautifully carved font cover can be seen in the church itself). On a more nautical note, tucked away in the undercroft is the barrel shaped crow's nest used by Sir Ernest Shakleton on his last Antarctic expedition.

Apsley House, The Wellington Museum

- 🖵 *149 Piccadilly, Hyde Park Corner, W1*
- 🕐 *0171 499 5676*
- 🚌 *Transport: Hyde Park Corner LU*
- 🕐 *Tues-Sun 11.00-17.00*
- ♨ *Admission £4 (adults), £2.50 (concessions)*
- 🛍 *Shop*
- ♿ *Limited access for visitors with disabilities*

The Waterloo Gallery, Apsley House

Home of the 1st Duke of Wellington, Apsley House (No. 1 London) must be the swankiest address in town. Its recently restored interiors are dressed to impress, gleaming with gilt and gold to reflect their owner's status as the hero of Waterloo. His many medals and orders can be admired in the basement gallery, along with a changing display of the (often vicious) satirical cartoons the Duke inspired. Military honours brought material gain, and the house positively groans under the weight of lavish gifts from grateful heads of state. Commemorative porcelain and silver dinner services crowd the cabinets of the Plate and China Room while the staircase is dominated by Canova's deeply kitsch nude statue of Napoleon (apparently even the Emperor himself was embarrassed by the outsized sculpture and banished it to the Louvre).

Many of the paintings on show came from the Spanish Royal Collection, among them Velasquez's justly famous 'Waterseller of Seville'. Elsewhere in the vast Waterloo Gallery earthy Dutch and Flemish genre scenes, like Jan Steen's bawdy 'Egg Dance' rub shoulders with devotional subjects like van Dyck's 'Saint Rosalie' and Correggio's 'Agony in the Garden' – a strange mix which makes for interesting viewing. Paintings of Wellington's comrades in arms hang in the ultra masculine environment of the Striped Drawing Room and include Lawrence's stirring portrait of him, looking every inch the Iron Duke.

The Bank of England Museum

- 🏛 *Threadneedle Street, EC2*
  (entrance in Bartholomew Lane)
- 🕿 *0171 601 5545*
- 🚌 *Transport: Bank LU*
- 🕐 *Mon-Fri 10.00-17.00*
- 🦋 *Admission free*
- 📖 *Shop*

What better place to get a handle on monetary matters than at the Old Lady of Threadneedle Street herself? The museum tells the story of the bank from its foundation in the late C17th and, like many an old institution, its history is a flamboyant one – on Wednesdays the gatekeeper is resplendent in full C17th

livery and up until 1971 the bank had its own military guard.

Displays trace the development of banking practice from goldsmiths' receipt notes through to electronic dealing, and include a full-sized reconstruction of Sir John Soane's C18th banking hall and one of the earliest surviving cheques (dated 8th December 1660). Gold bullion and one of the millions of quill pens that the Bank's clerks in the C19th got through every year can be found in the 1930's style Rotunda. The Coin and Paper Money galleries display some fine examples of the money-maker's art, including the master drawings for some recent bank notes.

Interactive computers are a feature of the contemporary banking displays and, with quickfire question and answer sessions, offer proactive participation. If you're feeling flush following a go on the foreign exchange computer game, treat yourself to a Britannia 4 Gold Proof Set of coins (a snip at around £1,175) in the museum shop (losers can console themselves with chocolate money).

The Banqueting House

- 🏛 *Whitehall, SW1*
- 🕿 *0171 930 4179 (booking)*
- 🕿 *0171 839 8919 (general information)*
- 🚌 *Transport: Westminster LU,*
  Charing Cross LU, Embankment LU
- 🕐 *Mon-Sat 10.00-17.00*
- 🦋 *Admission £3.25 (adults), £2.50 (senior*
  citizen/students), £2.15 (under 16s)
- 📖 *Shop*

Architecturally distinguished and graced with some typically fleshy ceiling paintings by Rubens, the Banqueting House's place in history is assured by virtue of having been the venue for the execution of King Charles I in 1649. (Rather more a chop house than banqueting hall then?)

Bramah Tea & Coffee Museum

- *The Clove Building, Maguire Street, SE1*
- *0171 378 0222*
- *Transport: London Bridge LU, Tower Hill LU*
- *Mon-Sun 10.00-18.00*
- *Admission £3.50 (adults),*
  £2.00 (concessions)
- *Shop*
- *Cafe*
- *Wheelchair access*

This quirky celebration of tea and coffee (two of London's historic trades) is a good antidote to the measured slickness of the nearby Design Museum. The Bramah's makeshift air is rather endearing and, providing you can overlook the typos in the wall labels and haphazard displays, offers an enjoyable trawl through the history of Britain's favourite brews.

The tea exhibits cover everything from the Chinese origins of Camellia Sinensis to tea cosies, via the stories of the Dutch and English trading companies who helped to turn Britain into a nation of tea drinkers. Old prints depicting the tea industry and scenes from the C18th 'tea and leisure' gardens evoke earlier periods of tea drinking, and a vast collection of teapots includes the world's largest, specially commissioned by the museum's founder Edward Bramah. Despite its sober image, there is a racier side to the humble cuppa. The museum looks at the connection between opium and tea, and even solves the knotty question of whether to put milk in first or last.

Coffee gets shorter shrift, although the machinery associated with its manufacture and preparation is much more impressive. A dizzying variety of percolators, filters, cafetiéres and hulking chrome-clad espresso machines testify to an inspired search for the perfect infusion. Displays chart the fluctuating fortunes of coffee drinking in this country, from early coffee houses such as Lloyds, through to the craze for coffee bars in the 50's and the infamous rise of coffee granules (cunningly designed for commercial breaks on television and quickly countered by the development of the tea bag).

The museum's own Tea and Coffee Room operates a stringent no tea bag or instant coffee policy but does allow visitors to sample the Real McCoy, surrounded by satirical C18th prints by Hogarth and Gillray. The small shop stocks several kinds of 'slow-infusing' teas and freshly roasted and ground coffees.

British Dental Association Museum

- *64 Wimpole Street, W1*
- *0171 935 0875*
- *Transport: Bond Street LU, Oxford Circus*
  LU, Regent's Park LU
- *Mon-Fri 10.00-16.00*
- *Admission free*

Presided over by the image of Apollonia, patron saint of toothache, this is probably not the museum to visit en route to the dentist. Serried ranks of extractors, drills, probes and syringes of varying antiquity and savagery await the visitor, along with mouthfuls of artificial teeth and dentures from the C18th to the present. Dental cartoons and a display of larger equipment (X-ray machines, anaesthetic units and dental chairs), from the C16th century barber's chair to the sophisticated late Victorian 'Morrison' chair – trace the emergence of dentistry as a modern profession. For royal watchers there's also a velvet upholstered dentist's chair from Buckingham Palace and a spittoon stand from Queen Victoria's dentist.

British Museum

- ⌨ *Great Russell Street, WC1*
- ☏ *0171 636 1555*
- ☏ *0171 580 1788 (recorded information);*
- ☏ *0171 637 7384 (recorded information for people with disabilities)*
- 🚌 *Transport: Holborn LU, Russell Square LU, Tottenham Court Road LU*
- 🕐 *Mon-Sat 10.00-17.00, Sun 12.00-18.00*
- 💰 *Admission Free (a charge maybe made for temporary exhibitions)*
- ✎ *Shop, Bookshop, Café*
- ♿ *Disabled Access*

The ultimate perch for culture vultures. Established by an act of Parliament in 1753 and occupying a majestic 13½ acre site in Bloomsbury, the BM is for many the quintessential London museum. With some 6½ million artifacts and 90 odd galleries contained behind its Greek-temple-on-steroids facade the BM is far too big a beast to do justice in this review –

or indeed in a single foot-slogging visit. Both should rather be regarded as an appetizer to a multi-course banquet; like most big museums, the BM is better suited to regular visits. Free floor plans are available from the information desk in the main entrance hall but as both the main shop and bookshop are housed just off here, this area can get extremely congested. If you're planning to visit galleries on the north side of the building (eg. Prints and Drawings, Oriental Collections, Antiquities from Egypt) you may prefer to use the quieter, less well known Montague Place entrance (just off Gower Street).

Once inside, where to start? For first timers, the free introductory 'Eye Opener' tours are a painless way to find your feet – each tour lasts about an hour and topics include 'The World of Asia', 'Early Egypt and Nubia' and 'Europe: Medieval to Modern'. 90 minute guided tours of the museum's highlights cost £6 and should be

The Dying lioness. A Gypsum carving from the palace of Ashurbanipal at Nineveh.

booked at the Information Desk; illustrated souvenir guide books come in at £5. For those going solo personal preference will no doubt dictate your route but, if you're feeling strong, start with the perennially popular Egyptian galleries. Plough your way through the crowds of clipboard-carrying kids hell bent on answering the next question on their activity sheets (available from the Information Desk) and admire instead the inscrutable beauty – despite the broken noses – of the colossal Egyptian and Assyrian sculptures on the ground floor (rooms 26 and 25), and the world class collection of antiquities from Egypt on the upper floor (galleries 61-66). Pride of place in the sculpture galleries goes not to a statue but to the Rosetta Stone – a undistinguished-looking stone slab whose multilingual inscriptions helped crack the 'code' of hieroglyphics. In the upper floor galleries the evolution of Egyptian make-up palettes speaks volumes about the long term benefits of wearing eye liner but, among a whole host of thousands of years old artefacts and funerary finds, the real crowd pleasers here are the mummies – human as well as animal – and their richly decorated coffins. A particularly well preserved corpse from 3400 BC, curled up and surrounded by essentials for the after-life (a make-up palette), is apparently one of the most popular exhibits in the whole museum – you can even buy a post card of it from the shop.

Ancient Egyptian attitudes to life and death will be explored in a suite of new galleries called Eyptian Funerary Archaeology, opening in 1999. If ancient civilisations are your thing, don't miss The Raymond and Beverly Sackler Galleries (rooms 53-56) which cover Ancient Anatolia, and Early and Later Mesopotamia and whose exhibits include finds from Ninevah and Babylon, such as the justly famous relief carving of a dying lion and part of a 3,000 year old thesaurus.

The museum is also well endowed with antiquities and sculpture from ancient Greece and Rome. On the ground floor room 8 is devoted to sculptures from the Parthenon (aka the Elgin Marbles). Leaving aside the knotty issue of repatriation, these are marvels of craftsmanship and artistry, from the lovingly depicted tunics of the gods in the pediments to the action packed frieze showing the Panathenaic procession parading around the room – at eye level, luckily. Another ancient structure, the Lykein tomb – the first ever example of a temple tomb – is displayed in room 7 and more classical architectural odds and ends can be found in the basement (room 77) – including massive Ionic volutes from Ephesis and an elegantly draped caryatid from the Erectheum. There's plenty in the way of smaller artifacts like pottery and jewellery too – look out for the Portland Vase, a stunning example of Roman cameo work (room 70). Gallery 69 provides a kaleidoscope of insights into the daily life of the inhabitants of the ancient world – from childhood to chariot racing, drinking to divorce (as illustrated by a set of divorce papers from 96AD), and trade to transport.

Still on a Roman theme, the recently opened Weston Gallery of Roman Britain (room 49) is a beautifully displayed collection of artifacts from the Roman Occupation. Much of the display focuses on the Roman military presence: cavalry armour, a bronze army diploma and so on – but some of the most exciting exhibits are the hoards of treasure that have been unearthed over the years. The Thetford Treasure of late Roman jewellery includes some amazingly flamboyant finger rings while the elegant silver tableware from the Hoxne hoard and Mildenhall treasures bespeak the ultimate in gracious living. Not to be outdone by the corpses elsewhere in the museum, room 50 (Later Bronze Age and Celtic Europe) is home to Lindow man – a sacrificial victim from the first century AD, preserved for posterity in a peat bog until he was discovered a few years ago.

Moving through European history, the Medieval, Renaissance and Modern collection use applied arts to chart the dramatic social, religious and political changes of the era. The wonderfully gnomic C12th Lewis Chessmen can be tracked down in room 42 but the diffuse range of artifacts goes right up to the C20th with a few curiosities like Lord Palmerston's garter and Napoleon's death mask thrown in for good measure. The march of time can be seen literally in the display of clocks and watches in room 44. The BM's horological collection is the most comprehensive in existence and it's worth arriving on the hour to hear, amongst others, the harmonious chime of Nicholas Villon's C16th carillon clock. The newly opened HSBC Money gallery (room 68) examines another great imponderable but takes an even longer view – exploring the history of money over the past 4,000 years and charting the development of coins, notes, electronic money and the systems which regulate them.

Flagging yet? Perhaps it's time for a coffee and a bite to eat. The museum's self service café serves appetising hot and cold food but is small considering the size of the museum and amount of visitors it attracts per year. If culture-induced claustrophobia has set in, investigate some of the excellent small caffs in the area. Museum Street has a few including the incomparable Museum Street Coffee Gallery (superior cakes, coffees and Italian food). Pizza Express (corner of Coptic Street and Little Museum Street) and Wagamama (Streatham Street) are safe bets for more substantial meals.

Sutton Hoo Buckle

Ease back gently into the fray with a post-prandial potter around room 90, which hosts temporary exhibitions organised by the Prints and Drawings Department. Manageable in size but of high quality, these are usually worth a separate visit – past shows have included French avant-garde printmaking, Islamic and Indian miniatures, and graphic work from Scandinavia.

Further up the North Stairs the exquisite Japanese galleries display selections from the BM's collection of Japanese arts and crafts. With material dating from the prehistoric Jumon period to the Heisei era (1989 onwards), the displays are regularly changed because of the delicate organic materials from which most Japanese cultural artifacts are made, so it's a good idea to telephone or consult the BM's Events leaflet before setting out to check galleries won't be closed for rearrangement. The wooden tea house is a permanent feature but other exhibits might include razor sharp samurai swords, delicately carved netsuke, painted scrolls and screens and Ukiyo-e prints and books. These galleries lead downstairs to The Arts of Korea, a temporary display of the arts and archaeology of Korea and forerunner to a permanent Korean gallery scheduled to open in the former map room of the British Library in 2000.

With a fine sense of understatement the museum's Plans and Information leaflet identifies the Indian sculpture in room 33 as an "object of special interest". In fact the whole of this vast and absorbing gallery (also just off the North Stairs) covers China as well as South and Southeast Asia and among its jumble of exhibits are ritual vessels, Tang dynasty tomb pottery figures, statues from Jain temples, snuff bottles, buddhas galore, Vietnamese ceramics and much more besides. Tucked away at the far end, Room 33a is home to a selection of relief carvings depicting scenes from the life of Buddha from the Great Stupa at Amaravati, while just off the Montague Place entrance the John Addis Gallery of Islamic Art contains graphic art, weaponry and an extensive display of colourful and intricately patterned Iznik and Damascus tiles.

Although just a few years shy of its 250th anniversary, and still Britain's most visited museum, the BM is not about to sit on its laurels now. The 'Great Court Scheme' currently under way (and scheduled for completion in 2000) promises a radical transformation of the space vacated by the British Library in its move to St Pancras. A sanctuary for generations of scholars, the round Reading Room will become an open access library specialising in cultures represented by the museum while the surrounding courtyard, hidden from view since 1857, will be opened up to provide a 2 acre square for exhibitions and displays. Even more exciting is the return of the Ethnographic department to Bloomsbury after years of exile at the Museum of Mankind (closed at the end of 1997), and the provision of permanent galleries for the African, American, Pacific, European and Asian collections in addition to the Mexican gallery already in situ (room 33c).

While visitors in the 21st Century can expect greatly enhanced facilities, museum-goers will in the meantime have to put up with disruptions to facilities and events such as the popular lunchtime lectures. A more worrying development is the very real threat of admission charges hanging over this great institution. True, other once free museums in London now charge but, financial crisis or no, the introduction of entrance fees at the BM would surely be a retrogressive step – and one which ran counter to the wishes of benefactors who bequeathed objects on the understanding that admission was free. Thankfully, the museum's trustees have decided that free admission will continue – at least until 1999 – and let's hope the BM is able to continue this enlightened tradition long into the 21st century. If not, make the most of it while you can.

The Cabinet War Rooms

🖼 *Clive Steps, King Charles Street, SW1*
📞 *0171 930 6961*
🚌 *Transport: Westminster LU,
St James's Park LU*
🕐 *Daily 9.30-18.00
(10.00-18.00, 1 October-31 March)*
🏛 *Admission £4.40 (adults), £2.20 (children/
unemployed), £3.30 (OAPs/students)*
🛍 *Shop*
♿ *Wheelchair access*

Winston Churchill and his ministers spent much of WWII holed up in these underground offices, for six years a secret nerve centre for the British government and military top brass. Preserved as an historic site since 1948 and still sporting original fixtures and fittings (although now staffed by a few mannequins), the CWR are a spookily atmospheric time capsule of the years 1939-40.

Built to withstand the Nazi Blitzkrieg, the CWR now surrender themselves daily to armies of visitors who file past rooms

The Transatlantic Telephone Room

where history was made: the converted broom cupboard from which Churchill telephoned Roosevelt, the Prime Minister's spartan office-cum-bedroom, the Map Room, as well as the inner sanctum of the whole complex – the Cabinet Room itself. Less glamourous rooms like the typing pool evoke the drudgery of war work and there are displays examining different aspects of the war. The tour ends on a lighter note with an exhibition of caricatures of wartime personalities by the cartoonist Sallon.

Free audio guides in a range of languages are issued on arrival and lasting 1 hour, are essential listening for visitors who wish to explore the site thoroughly. Shorter guides are available for those with less time and there's a children's version for the under 11's. Although there's no café on site, the shop doesn't ration the souvenirs, stocking a good selection of goods with a wartime theme.

Chartered Insurance Institute Museum

🖼 *The Hall, 20 Aldermanbury, EC2*
📞 *0171 417 4425*
🚌 *Transport: Moorgate LU, Bank LU,
St Paul's LU*
🕐 *Mon-Fri 9.00-17.00*
🏛 *Admission free (phone in advance if possible)*

Perhaps not the most scintillating premise for a museum, but this well ordered one-room display nevertheless succeeds in making the history of insurance interesting. Fire insurance seems to be the main focus but life, marine, motor and accident cover are also examined and there are some wonderfully florid early policies on show.

Fire insurance only really took off in Britain after the Great Fire of London. A C19th horse-drawn fire engine takes pride of place among the exhibits, along with some early fireman's helmets and buckets, and tokens given to volunteer pumpers to be exchanged for a pint of beer.

The Clink Museum

🖃 *1 Clink Street, SE1*
🕾 *0171 378 1558*
🚍 *Transport: London Bridge LU*
🕙 *Mon-Sun 10.00-18.00*
🏷 *Admission £3.50 (adults), £2.50 (under 15's/concessions), £8.00 (families)*
🛍 *Shop*

This exhibition, built on the site of the original Clink prison, is more an attraction than a museum. Although a variety of authentic torture instruments are displayed, perhaps the most painful feature of the museum is having to read the typos in the wall labels. Tableaux depict the less than appealing aspects of life in the clink and, for those keen to experience the harsh character of an earlier criminal justice system more closely, some exhibits like the weighty ball and chain are hands on.

The Design Museum

🖃 *Shad Thames, SE1*
🕾 *0171 378 6055*
🚍 *Transport: London Bridge LU, Tower Bridge LU*
🕙 *Mon-Fri 11.30-18.00; Sat-Sun 12.00-18.00*
🏷 *Admission £5.25 (adults), £4.00 (children), £12.00 (families)*
🛍 *Shop*
🍽 *Cafés*
♿ *Wheelchair access*

Funded in part by the Conran Foundation, this museum, as its title implies, is a shrine to design. Its riverside home, a sleek white building in 1930's cruise liner style, stands in stark contrast to the historic red brick shipping warehouses of Shad Thames.

However, inside the museum's focus is more 'homage to the homely', with an emphasis on domestic items like washing machines and televisions. The spacious top floor gallery boasts a superb panoramic view of the north bank of the Thames and houses the 'Collection', an exploration of design for mass-produced goods. The displays here are arranged thematically with entire cases devoted to one type of product tracing, say, the history of the angle poise lamp or fountain pen. An arrangement of kettles illustrates how social, cultural, technological and economic factors influence a product's design (and you thought it was just something for boiling water). In a refreshing reversal of the roped-off chair scenario of many museums, this gallery features a row of different designer chairs for visitors to sit on – making it possible to test drive a sedentary icon like Gerrit Rietveld's 'Red/Blue Chair' of 1918.

On the floor below, the smaller 'Review' gallery offers a changing survey of new designs and includes preliminary drawings and models as well as actual prototypes. On my visit exhibits ranged from a tubular bus stop to mineral water bottles to trainers.

The museum's displays are quite concise (in a modern, uncluttered kind of way, naturally), but confirmed style junkies shouldn't worry. Both the Review and Collection galleries hold changing temporary displays and exhibitions – future shows look set to include vehicle designs by Porsche and the work of industrial designer, David Mellor.

For aesthetic gratification of the take home variety, the museum shop carries tempting designer knick-knacks from Muji stationery to Philippe Starck furniture. The book selection is equally eclectic with glossy lifestyle coffee table tomes jostling for supremacy over more technical titles like 'Glass Reinforced Plastics in Construction'. The foyer coffee shop offers light refreshments while the Conran-run Blueprint Cafe is also on site for those with more sophisticated tastes and larger wallets.

MUSEUMS - CENTRAL

The Design Museum

The Dickens House Museum

- ▭ *48 Doughty Street, WC1*
- ◔ *0171 405 2127*
- ⊞ *Transport: Russell Square LU*
- ◷ *Mon-Sat 10.00-17.00*
- ✈ *Admission £3.50 (Adults) £2.50 (Students) £1.50 (Children) £7 (families)*
- ✎ *Shop*

Although Charles Dickens only lived at this address for little more than two years, the house has become something of a shrine to the writer who gave us 'Oliver Twist', 'David Copperfield' and 'The Pickwick Papers'. With its pea green paintwork and lino floorings, the house is a suitably quirky repository of Dickensania and likely to appeal to confirmed fans only.

Displays includes fragments of original manuscripts and a variety of odds and ends connected with the great man – anything, it seems, from his well-worn writing desk to a lemon squeezer! Ironically for such a literary haunt, many exhibits are highly visual. Numerous illustrations to Dickens' books, and portraits of the writer by eminent Victorians such as W. P. Frith and the gloriously named Augustus Egg are on show.

The library in the basement holds a bewildering variety of Dickens editions, and although it's the last room on the tour suggested by the guidebook, its excellent potted history video makes it well worth stopping here first. The small shop stocks antiquarian and new editions of Dickens' oeuvre as well as the sort of kitsch which seems to be an inevitable element in the destiny of great writers from the Bard onwards – this is the place to pick up a handy 'Pickwick Quill' or that useful brass toasting fork you've always wanted.

Diocesan Treasury

- ▭ *The Crypt, St Paul's Cathedral, EC4*
- ◔ *0171 246 8348*
- ⊞ *Transport: St Paul's LU*
- ◷ *Crypt open: Mon-Sat 8.45-16.00*
- ✈ *Admission£3.50 (Adults), £2.00 (Children), £3.00 (Concessions)*
- ✎ *Shop*
- ♿ *Wheelchair access (via southern transept)*

Once you're done gazing at the splendid interior of Wren's masterpiece, a look around the crypt is a good antidote to the cricked neck you've probably acquired (admission is included in the entrance ticket to the Cathedral). A glittering display of altar plate is accompanied by insights into how Reformation shenanigans affected its design, and there are some beautiful examples of the embroiderer's art. These include the 'Jubilee Cope', whose gold thread decorations depict in loving detail the spires of no less than 73 London churches. Elsewhere in the crypt are the tombs of Britain's illustrious dead – Wellington and Nelson among them – and of course, the cathedral's architect himself, Sir Christopher Wren (See pages 17, 38, 69, 76 and 84).

The Florence Nightingale Museum

- *St Thomas' Hospital,*
  2 Lambeth Palace Road, SE1
- *0171 620 0374*
- *Transport: Westminster LU,*
  Waterloo LU, Lambeth North LU
- *Tues-Sun 10.00-17.00*
- *Admission £2.50 (adults),*
  £1.50 (concessions), £5 (families)
- *Shop*
- *Wheelchair access*

A legend in her own lifetime, Florence Nightingale was much more than simply 'The Lady with the Lamp', as this museum shows. Beginning with her unfulfilled, privileged youth, it follows Florence's remarkable career through the bloodshed of the Crimean War to the energetic campaigning for health reform which occupied the remainder of her life.

Witty, intelligent, shrewd and single-minded, this ministering angel didn't mind putting a few backs up to achieve her goals, and the museum takes a commendably even-handed approach to the complexities of its subject. Some of the displays err on the side of wordiness but most of the relevant facts can be gleaned (in the comfort of the small cinema) from the audio visual show.

Original letters, nurses' uniforms and Miss Nightingale's Crimean medicine chest are among the personal artifacts on show, along with the shell of 'Jimmy', the pet tortoise at Scutari hospital. A selection of affordable souvenirs and a variety of books about nursing are available at the shop, and refreshments are served on the hospital site.

The Florence Nightingale Museum

The Golden Hinde

- St Mary Overie Dock, Cathedral Street, SE1
- 0171 403 0123
- 0541 50504 (school bookings)
- Transport: London Bridge LU
- Phone for opening times
- Admission £2.30 (Adults)
  £1.50 (children)
- Shop

The Golden Hinde

This part of London is so steeped in history that it comes as little surprise to see this full-sized replica of Sir Francis Drake's C16th warship moored up near Southwark Cathedral. Although describing itself as a 'museum ship', the brightly coloured vessel has clocked up over 100,000 miles and with its neatly-trimmed rigging and sturdy structure, still feels very much like a working ship.

Armed with a tour leaflet, the visitor has a pretty free run of the ship – from the depths of the hold, to the cramped gun deck and up to Drake's cabin (the only private one on board). A few sea chests and barrels aside, there's not much in the way of décor and below decks low ceilings and steep stairs make the going difficult for grown ups. Nonetheless it's pretty atmospheric and children should enjoy the challenging terrain. Guided tours are available for groups.

Grand Lodge Library and Museum

- Freemasons' Hall, Great Queen Street, WC2
- 0171 831 9811
- Transport: Holborn LU, Covent Garden LU
- Mon-Fri 10.00-17.00, Sat 10.00-13.00
- Admission free
- Shop
- Wheelchair access

While this museum and permanent exhibition doesn't spill the beans on funny handshakes and rolled-up trouser legs, it does shed a glimmer of light on the elusive yet high profile organisation that is Freemasonry.

Housed in the intimidatingly expansive Freemasons' Hall (erected in the 1930's), the museum is itself pretty cavernous. Case after case displays the United Grand Lodge's extensive collection of masonic glass, china and silverware from lodges around the world. Insignia and regalia are also much in evidence, and with names like 'the Order of the Secret Monitor' the masons' reputation for clandestine practice seems understandable. Documents include the minutes and accounts books kept by PoW masons at Stalag 383, Nuremburg and a letter congratulating Queen Victoria on her escape from an assassination attempt.

The permanent exhibition broadly charts the 'history of English Freemasonry and its development from medieval obscurity to world-wide prominence' but, again, without giving too much away. Portraits and photographs of masons include those of Elias Ashmole, the C17th founder of Oxford's Ashmolean Museum, Alexander Fleming (see p.74) and Peter Sellers. Among the unusual artifacts on display are an outsized Grand Master's throne and a beautifully hand-embroidered masonic apron from the C18th. Books, videos and various regalia are available from The Grand Charity's souvenir shop on the ground floor.

The Grand Temple vestibule ceiling, Grand Lodge Library and Museum

Grant Museum of Zoology and Comparative Anatomy

- ⌨ *Darwin Building, UCL, Gower Street, WC1*
- ☎ *0171 504 2647*
- 🚌 *Transport: Euston LU, Warren St LU, Euston Square LU, Goodge Street LU*
- 🕐 *Mon-Fri 9.00-17.30 by appointment*
- 🎟 *Admission Free*
- ♿ *Wheelchair access (ring in advance)*

Many rare and extinct species can be seen in this natural history collection. Founded in 1828, this is one of the very oldest natural history collections, and with around 35,000 specimens it's not small either.

Great Ormond Street Hospital for Children NHS Trust Museum

- ⌨ *55 Great Ormond Street, WC1*
- ☎ *0171 405 9200 ext. 5920*
- 🚌 *Transport: Holborn LU, Russell Square LU*
- 🕐 *Mon-Fri 9.30-16.00 by appointment*
- 🎟 *Admission free*

Exhibits illustrating the history of the hospital, together with the Peter Pan Collection – books from around the world about Never Never Land's ever-youthful resident.

The Guards Museum

- ⌨ *Wellington Barracks, Birdcage Walk, SW1*
- ☎ *0171 414 3271*
- 🚌 *Transport: St James Park LU*
- 🕐 *Daily 10.00-16.00*
- 🎟 *Admission £2 (adults), £1 (children, OAP's, ex-Guardsmen), £4 (families)*
- 🛍 *Shop*
- ♿ *Wheelchair access (telephone in advance)*

The history of the five regiments of foot guards – the Grenadier, Coldstream, Scots, Irish and Welsh Guards – in one museum. With their distinctive scarlet tunics and bearskin hats, guards are perhaps best known for their ceremonial role in the capital but have also played their part in Britain's numerous military campaigns. Uniforms include a guard's tunic worn by Edward VIII, the Grand Old Duke of York's bearskin and a Dervish chain mail shirt, while among the more unusual exhibits are souvenirs from the Battle of Waterloo, a device for tattooing deserters and the wicker picnic basket used by Field Marshal Montgomery while on a campaign in Italy. For visitors inspired to play war games, the Toy Soldier Centre is close at hand to supply battalions of tiny tin troops and a selection of vintage tin toy farm animals.

Guildhall Clock Museum

- ⌨ *Guildhall, Aldermanbury, EC2*
- ☎ *0171 606 3030 ext 1460*
- 🚌 *Transport: St Paul's LU, Moorgate LU, Bank LU, Mansion House LU*
- 🕐 *Mon-Fri 9.30-16.45*
- 🎟 *Admission free*
- ♿ *Wheelchair access*

Time waits for no one – especially here, at the Museum of the Worshipful Company of Clockmakers, where some 700 clocks and watches testify to man's ingenious attempts over the centuries to keep tabs on this most slippery of concepts. Some unusual timepieces lurk amongst the more elegant pocket watches and stately longcase clocks – like a macabre silver skull watch reputedly owned by Mary Queen of Scots and an innocuous-looking device which turns out to be the timer for an early nuclear weapon. There are also examples of John 'Longitude' Harrison's award-winning work (time really is money) and a state of the art Patek Philippe wristwatch movement from 1990, which features a revolutionary 'escapement'.

The Hahneman Relics

- Hahneman House, 2 Powis House, Great Ormond Street WC1
- 0171 713 6280
- Transport: Russell Square LU, Holborn LU
- Visits by prior appointment
- Admission free

The museum displays the artifacts belong to Dr Samuel Hahneman and his disciples and is available for those interested in homeopathy. While Hahneman House is being renovated, the museum will not be open to the public until the first quarter of 1998.

HMS Belfast

- Morgans Lane, Tooley Street, SE1
- 0171 407 6434
- Transport: London Bridge LU, Tower Hill LU, Monument, LU
- Daily 10.00-18.00 (1 March-31 October 10.00-17.00)
- Admission £4.70 (adults), £2.40 (children), £3.60 (concessions)
- Shop
- Café
- Partial wheelchair access

Weighing in at 11,553 tonnes, HMS Belfast is Europe's largest big-gun armoured warship to have survived from WWII, and the first warship to be preserved for the nation since Nelson's Victory. Moored just upstream of Tower Bridge, she is boarded via a gangplank on the South bank but can be exited more picturesquely, by a ferry to Tower Pier on the North bank.

Once on board there's a lot of ground to cover but be prepared for low-slung doorways and steep ladders. For ease of orientation the ship is divided into eight zones and the entry ticket comprises a handy map (even so, I still managed to go adrift and miss out on several rooms). Rather more sophisticated navigational tools can be seen on the Bridge, home of the Compass Platform and the wireless office (restored and now manned by an amateur radio society).

Although she hasn't fired a shot in anger since the Korean War, HMS Belfast's big guns are still very much in evidence on the upper decks, while deep below the waterline are the claustrophobic shell rooms. In service from 1938-1966, the ship has not been preserved with reference to just one moment in time, but instead reflects her lengthy career – the ship's log is open at D-Day and while the operations room reconstructs key moments of the Battle of North Cape with life-like mannequins and soundtrack, the mess decks with their bakery, canteen, dormitory, sickbay and operating theatre show how HMS Belfast looked after her 1950's refit.

A permanent exhibition 'HMS Belfast in War and Peace' fleshes out the portrait of the ship and those who served aboard her, charting her career from her building and launch in 1938 with contemporary paintings, photographs, plans, artifacts and not one but four historical videos. Another permanent display, 'The Modern Royal Navy' provides a wider context – even if it does feel a bit like a recruiting exercise.

In both menu and ambience, the ship's Walrus Café favours function over charisma but back on dry land the museum shop offers some consolation: model boat kits, HMS Belfast ties and a small fleet of books on naval subjects.

House of Detention

- *Clerkenwell Close, EC1*
- *0171 253 9494*
- *Transport: Farringdon LU*
- *Daily 10.00-18.00*
- *Admission £4 (adults), £3 (Students/OAPs), £2.50 (children), £10 (families)*

Not an S&M joint, but one of London's more macabre attractions. Once the capital's busiest gaol the House of Detention now offers visitors a taste of crime and punishment, Victorian style. The gloomy underground vaults – all that remains of the actual gaol – are undeniably creepy and contain reconstructions of the C19th fumigation room, kitchen and laundry (complete with hammy soundtrack). Although the cells are the real thing, there's not much else in the way of exhibits, apart from some stomach-turning torture instruments and medical equipment. While it is at present rather basic, there are plans to build a café and shop, as well as to open up further corridors and cells sealed since 1890.

Imperial War Museum

- *Lambeth Road, SE1*
- *0171 416 5000*
- *Transport: Lambeth North LU, Elephant and Castle LU, Waterloo LU*
- *Mon-Sun 10.00-18.00*
- *Admission £4.70 (Adults), £2.35 (Children), £12.50 (Adults), £3.50 (Concessions), free after 16.30*
- *Shop*
- *Café*
- *Wheelchair access*

War is often described as a kind of madness, so it's perhaps appropriate that a museum dedicated to C20th conflict should be housed in the former lunatic asylum known as Bedlam. The subject of an ongoing redevelopment programme,

Imperial War Museum

the facilities and displays are top notch, taking visitors beyond just the instruments of war to focus on people – both the perpetrators and the victims of conflict. The lofty entrance hall is dominated by the bulky hardware of modern warfare: aeroplanes, tanks, jeeps, rockets and a WW1 German periscope mast, so powerful that through it you can see the dome of St Paul's, 2 miles away.

A permanent exhibition examining C20th warfare occupies the lower ground floor and is divided into four parts: WW1, the inter-war years, WWII and post-war conflicts. Displays within each section are thematic rather than strictly chronological, reducing a vast, potentially daunting subject into manageable chunks. As well as artifacts such as uniforms, equipment and weaponry, important historical documents are also displayed: letters and manuscripts from WW1 poets and, more chillingly, Adolf Hitler's fateful directive ordering the invasion of Poland.

Personal artifacts from both well-known and anonymous soldiers shift the emphasis from the political to the personal. Recorded eyewitness accounts can be accessed through headsets while archive footage of specific battles helps recreate an accurate picture of events. (Only a small proportion of the museum's extensive collection of film, sound recordings, photographs and documents can be shown, but reference facilities are available by appointment). Many displays – such as that dealing with the liberation of Bergen Belsen concentration camp, and PoW's in the Far East – are distressing. The trench and Blitz participatory displays are presumably designed for the benefit of those too young to remember the real thing and, in a kind of hand-it-to-you-on-a plate way, work reasonably well – although some people may find the 'experience' rather too voyeuristic for comfort.

Upstairs, 'The Secret War' dishes the dirt on Britain's spies and has no end of nifty gadgets. Ian Fleming's 'Q' would have been chuffed with the interactive computers which let visitors sift through the files of various real life agents and spill the beans on their missions. On the same floor, the Victoria Cross and George Cross Gallery commemorates the bravery of individual soldiers and civilians with a display of over 40 medals and associated memorabilia.

Saving the best for last, the museum's art collection is housed on the top floor and, with holdings of C20th art second only to those of the Tate Gallery, is worth a visit in its own right. Like the Tate, its art displays are changed periodically but expect to see works by Stanley Spencer, Paul Nash, Henry Moore and Graham Sutherland. John Singer Sargent's unforgettable depiction of WW1, 'Gassed' has been allocated a room of its own, where it hangs with his evocative wartime watercolours.

Inns of Court & City Yeomanry Museum

- 10 Stone Buildings, Lincolns Inn, WC2
- 0171 405 8112
- Transport: Chancery Lane LU
- Mon-Fri 10.00-16.00 (phone first)
- Admission free
- Shop

A military museum containing weapons, uniforms, equipment and original documents of the City of London Yeomanry and Inns of Court regiments from the Napoleonic era to the present day. The highlight of the collection is a rare and complete set of drums of the Law Association Volunteers, active between 1803 and 1808.

Dr Johnson's House

- 17 Gough Square, EC4
- 0171 353 3745
- Transport: Blackfriars LU, Chancery Lane LU
- Mon-Sat 11.00-17.30 (Oct-April 11.00-17.00)
- Admission £3 (adults), £2 (OAPs/students), £1 (children)
- Shop

It was in the garret of this early C18th house that Dr Samuel Johnson compiled his famous Dictionary: the first comprehensive lexicon of the English language. The house has been restored to the condition it was in during Johnson's 11 year occupancy (from 1748 to 1759) and retains many original features – including some drastic early crime prevention measures and an ingenious 'cellarette' in the dining room. Arranged over several floors, the house has no shortage of stairs, but then to quote the words of the friendly attendant, "the chairs are for sitting on, not gawping at".

The house has other unexpected surprises. A brick from the Great Wall of China is a tangible reminder of Johnson's unrealised ambition to visit it, while the garret is home to a model toy workshop presented to the house by firefighters in WWII. Books, paintings and memorabilia of Dr Johnson and his circle can be found throughout the house and as well as the free information sheets in each room there's an entertaining and informative video show. Cards and collections of Johnson's sayings and bon mots are available in the small shop. (Incidentally, a glance in a facsimile of the Dictionary reveals that the great man defined a museum as a 'a repository of learned curiosities').

Kirkaldy Testing Museum

- ▭ *99 Southwark Street, SE1 (entrance Prices St)*
- ☎ *01322 332195*
- 🚃 *Transport: Blackfriars LU, Waterloo LU, London Bridge LU*
- 🕐 *Visits by appointment*
- ✇ *Admission £2*

This museum celebrates three generations of the Kirkaldy family who worked in Southwark testing engineering and building materials from 1866-1965. Housed in the firm's Victorian works building, David Kirkaldy's original all-purpose testing machine is still in place. Some 48 feet long and able to apply a load of over 300 tonnes, it tested the steel used to build Sydney Harbour Bridge and parts of the Comet airliner. Visits last about 1½ hours and reveal how this extraordinary machine functioned and its role in developing quality control techniques for constructional materials.

London Fire Brigade Museum

- ▭ *Winchester House, 94a Southwark Bridge Road, SE1*
- ☎ *0171 587 2894*
- 🚃 *Transport: Borough LU*
- 🕐 *Mon-Fri, 2 tours daily, by appointment,*
- ✇ *Admission £3 (adults), £2 (under 14)*
- ✇ *Shop*

Comprising one of the most comprehensive collections of firefighting equipment in the country, it's probably just as well that admission to this museum is by guided tour only. Arranged chronologically, the exhibits chart the development of the London fire service from 1666 to the present day and include paintings, photographs, uniforms, models and medals, among which is one of only three George Crosses to have been presented to firefighters.

Equipment ranges from tree trunk watermains, leather hosepipes and early breathing apparatus (operated by a footpump!) to modern thermal imaging cameras. Larger appliances such as the C19th telescopic fire escape ladder and a horse drawn 'steamer' from 1885 (immaculate in its red and gold livery) are displayed in the former Brigade HQ engine room. Particularly fine paintings of firefighting during the Blitz can be seen in the room dedicated to WWII while the Overseas Room contains badges and helmets of fire brigades from around the world. The tours are as extensive and entertaining as the collection and, filled with tales of bravery and even the supernatural, last between 1-2 hours. The small but choice selection of gifts in the museum shop features firemen's helmet paperweights for £8, bronze firefighters at £60, and an excellent fire extinguisher water squirter for just £1.

MUSEUMS - CENTRAL

London Transport Museum

- 🗔 *Covent Garden Piazza, WC2*
- 🕔 *0171 836 8557 (24 hour information)*
- 🕔 *0171 379 6344 (bookings and events)*
- 🚇 *Transport: Covent Garden LU*
- 🕐 *Daily 10.00-18.00 (Fri 11.00-18.00)*
- 🎫 *Admission £4.95 (adults), £2.95 (under 15's/Concessions), £12.85 (families)*
- 🛍 *Shop*
- ☕ *Café*

Located amid the hubbub of the Piazza, and housed in a former flower market, the LTM is a must for train, tram and bus-spotters, or indeed any of the millions who travel by public transport in the capital each year. This light, airy building is filled with historic vehicles and machinery, telling the story of the development of London's transport system from 1800 to the present day.

Lumbering horse-drawn vehicles preface the display but quickly give way to the electric and motor-powered trams and buses which revolutionised transport in the capital. Sympathetically restored but retaining a slightly battered feel, the vehicles are all surprisingly atmospheric: climbing aboard, it's easy to imagine a real journey on the West Ham Borough tram in its smart 1910 livery. Old cars seem to bring out the nostalgic in everyone and these workhorses are no exception: the museum reverberates to excited cries of "I remember these...". Period newsreels top up the nostalgia levels with moving footage like the dismantling of the capital's decommissioned trams in the 1950's.

While the adults take a trip down memory lane, the kids can get stuck into the numerous hands on exhibits: no shortage of multilingual touch screens, working models, buttons to press and handles to turn here. Actors bring the exhibits to life – on my visit a C19th navvy clambered about in the replica section of an early Underground tunnel to help explain its construction. Simulators give old and young a chance to get behind the wheel of bus or tube and are a popular (not to mention addictive) attraction. 'Drive' a 1938 tube train, and then see how computers have transformed life for drivers on the Victoria Line.

From trade unions right down to the design of litter bins and bus stops, the museum explores every conceivable aspect of London's transport network. Although the hardware is the main attraction, neither the social impact of public transport nor contemporary environmental concerns have been forgotten (although with a daily deposit of 1,000 tonnes of horse manure, things weren't too rosy in the C19th either). Temporary exhibitions held in the Frank Pick and Ashfield Galleries upstairs give the museum the chance to show off its collection of original posters as well as to explore particular aspects of London transport in detail.

If all that travel builds up your appetite, the museum's 'Transport Café' provides a handy pit stop with reasonably priced sandwiches and hot and cold drinks. However, with the whole of Covent Garden and Neal Street at your fingertips, you may fancy somewhere a little less utilitarian. For those bringing their own food, a picnic area is provided within the museum itself so you can munch on your sarnies in the shadow of one of the world's earliest mass produced motor buses, the B-Type of 1910.

The museum's shop is fun although the selection of books is uninspiring, and with titles like 'Single or Return? The history of the Transport Salaried Staff's Association' seems to be aimed squarely at the enthusiast. Posters, postcards and any amount of improbable items emblazoned with Harry Beck's map of the Underground and the LT logo should satisfy the less anorakish, with models, games and Paddington Bear for younger visitors.

London Transport Museum

The Michael Faraday Museum and Laboratory

🖃 *21 Albemarle Street, W1*
📞 *0171 409 2992*
🚌 *Transport: Green Park LU*
🕙 *Mon-Fri 10.00-18.00*
💷 *Admission £1 (adults), 50p (concessions)*
♿ *Wheelchair access*

London bookbinder turned experimental scientist Michael Faraday is one of science's giants. His discovery of electromagnetic induction paved the way for today's electrical industries. The laboratory at the Royal Institution where he made many important finds has been restored and is now accompanied by a museum. Much original apparatus is displayed along with the first sample of Benzene (another of Faraday's discoveries), early batteries and an electric egg.

Museum of Garden History

- 🏛 St Mary-at-Lambeth,
  Lambeth Palace Road, SE1
- ☎ 0171 401 8865
- 🚌 Transport: Waterloo LU,
  Lambeth North LU, Westminster LU
- 🕐 Mon-Fri 10.30-16.00, Sun 10.30-17.00
  (closed from the 2nd Sunday in December
  to the 1st Sunday in March)
- 🍽 Admission free
- ☕ Café
- 🛍 Shop
- ♿ Wheelchair access

You don't have to be a horny-handed son or daughter of the soil to appreciate this museum. With its ecclesiastical setting and intricately planted knot garden, it's an oasis of verdant tranquility amid the turmoil of Lambeth Bridge Roundabout.

For those with green-fingered tendencies, there are displays about pioneer gardeners like the Lambeth-based Tradescants (after whom the museum garden is named) as well as a small shrine-like display to the high priestess of gardening, Gertrude Jekyll. Old gardening equipment is exhibited throughout and artifacts range from cast iron Victorian lawnmowers to glass cucumber straighteners and the nifty 1920's 'Acme Insecticide Puffer'.

Out in the well-tended garden the plants (all clearly labelled) vie for attention with the churchyard's illustrious dead – William Bligh (captain of the ill-fated Bounty) and Elias Ashmole (freemason, see p.19) are both buried here. Back inside, the shop stocks a wide range of gardening books and good quality gifts with a floral theme. Frequented by doughty horticultural ladies, the licensed café serves tasty savoury food and cakes, its air thick with talk of borders, bedding-out and bad backs.

Museum of London

- 🏛 London Wall, EC2
- ☎ 0171 600 0807 (24 hr information line)
  0171 600 3699
- 🚌 Transport: Barbican, Bank, St Paul's,
  Moorgate LU
- 🕐 Tues-Sat 10.00-17.50 (last admission
  5.30pm), Sun 12.00-17.50
- 🍽 Admission charge £4 (adults),
  £2 (concessions/children),
  £9.50 (families); (tickets valid for 3 months
  – entrance is free after 4.30pm)
- 🛍 Shop
- ☕ Café

Even if you think you know London like the back of your hand, the chances are that you'll see the city in a new light after a trip to the MoL. Newcomers to the capital could also do a lot worse than make this their first stop. Full both of artifacts and insight, the museum offers an excellent chronological overview of London's history from prehistoric riverside settlement to sprawling modern metropolis.

With over 2,000 years worth of politics, pestilence, fires and invasions there's a lot of ground for the visitor to cover and, with admirable foresight, the museum has devised a fast-track route through its galleries for those with limited time – or attention spans. By following the bright green lights of the 'Catwalk' it's possible to skim through the permanent collection in just 45 minutes – although add an extra half hour if you want to dip into any of the main galleries. Staging posts along the Catwalk mark each of the 13 periods of London's history covered by the museum, with at-a-glance vital statistics and a small capsule display of artifacts. Nifty touchscreen computers provide more detailed information about the period and emit a satisfying 'whooshing' time travel type noise into the bargain. Unfurl the first map of London in the Medieval section, listen to Samuel

A Roman Wall Painting, The Museum of London

Pepys' diary of the devastating Great Fire (accompanied by some rather jolly dancing skeletons) or learn how civil war wracked the city.

Although the Catwalk has its advantages and satisfies 'been there, done that' criteria, you'll miss some of the best exhibits if you follow it too closely. Tickets are valid for three months, so if you've got the time, a longer visit or a return trip will really allow you to savour London's history, and enjoy the many similarities between then and now. It's kind of reassuring (but a tad depressing too) to know that generations of Londoners have wrestled with the problems of pollution, poverty, unscrupulous developers and healthcare (the notorious Bethlem Hospital discharged its mentally ill patients into the community after a year, cured or not). And foodies may be pleased to learn that Roman London's cosmopolitan population also had a taste for food and wine imported from the Med.

Inevitably, some periods come to life more readily than others. I'm afraid for me, Dark Age London only too readily lived up to its name and elements of the C20th displays were a bit lacklustre. The display on Prehistoric London was, however, strangely compelling: 'A Stoke Newington Fireside' diorama indicates that the area has been 'up and coming' for a lot longer than commonly suspected while archaeological finds of woolly rhino and mammoth teeth in Whitehall and on the site of the Old Bailey make present residents seem dull in comparison.

In fact many of the best artifacts have been dug up from beneath the City – like the beautifully carved statues which once adorned the Roman Temple of Mithras or the menacing armoury of unused swords dredged up from the Thames where they were thrown as an offering to the gods. Some items were never intended to see the light of day – like the sparkling hoard of Elizabethan jewels found in Cheapside and the bizarre mummified chickens bricked up in a Highgate chimney by a C17th builder.

Themes such as transport, health and multiculturalism run through the displays but the individual traits of each period are also examined. For example, C18th London was characterised not only by considerable artistic achievement in music, art and literature but also by a craze for calico fabric that nearly ruined the domestic weaving industry. Period rooms are a highlight of the museum: domestic interiors and shop fronts recreate the lives of the capital's past inhabitants rich and poor. No slouches when it came to architecture, the Romans built the City Wall, parts of which remain and can be seen from a viewing platform in the museum. The panelled walls of C18th cells from Wellclose Square prison are etched with the innumerable inscriptions of long-departed residents, while a magnificent collection of Victorian shops underlines the consumerism of C19th Imperial Britain. Another attraction, the 'Great Fire Experience', enables visitors to eavesdrop on history by watching the blaze spread across London's timber-framed houses and listen to Pepys describe its terrible progress. Firewatchers from a different era helped save London from a similar fate this century, as shown in the gallery devoted to WWII which evokes life in London during the Blitz – right down to a claustrophobic air-raid shelter and Utility furniture. Headsets let you listen to Londoners recounting their experiences of London's darkest hour on tapes specially recorded for the Museum's oral archive.

The museum reckons two hours is long enough to explore the main galleries but if you want stick within that time you'll still need to be discriminating – it's easy to get bogged down reading the wordy wall labels. In addition to the permanent displays, the museum stages regular temporary exhibitions – recent ones have

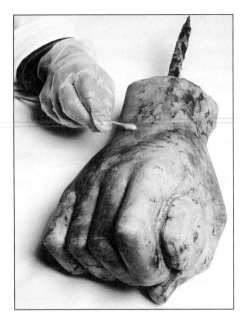

Hand of Mithras, Museum of London

included a celebration of 100 years of film-making in London – as well as organising a wide range workshops, talks, lectures and visits. Pick up a leaflet or ring the information line for details.

The Museum of London shop stocks a comprehensive range of books about London – from guidebooks and local history pamphlets to novels. The museum guide comes in two sizes, small (£2.95) and large (£7.95), and there are lots of general history books as well as an assortment of gifts and confectionery to supplements the literary offerings.

During the week this part of London – the corporate hub of the city – bristles with activity but a weekend visit finds the museum's environs much quieter. Luckily the museum has its own licensed café but chocoholics may prefer to take a short saunter along the high walk to the Barbican Centre's Waterside Café where a pretty mean chocolate brownie can be enjoyed beside the fountains and flowers.

The Museum of Methodism, Wesley's Chapel & House

- 49 City Road, EC1
- 0171 253 2262
- Transport: Old Street LU, Moorgate LU
- Mon-Sat 10.00-16.00, Sun 12.00-14.00
- Admission £4 (adults), £2 (concessions), £10 (families) free on Sundays
- Wheelchair access

"Perfectly neat but not fine" was how the founder of Methodism described the chapel he built in 1778, now known rather more grandly as the 'Cathedral of World Methodism'. The museum in the chapel's crypt tells the story of the Movement, with displays including Methodist art, ceramics and the electric shock machine used by Wesley to treat cases of depression. More conventional household effects belonging to Wesley can be seen in his house, across the courtyard from the chapel.

Museum of the Moving Image

- South Bank, Waterloo SE1
- 0171 401 2636 (recorded information)
- 0171 928 3232 (box office for screenings and events)
- Transport: Waterloo LU, Embankment LU
- Mon-Sun 10.00-18.00
- Admission £6.25 (adults), £5.25 (students), £4.50 (children/concessions)
- Shop
- Café
- Wheelchair access

Inelegantly huddled beneath Waterloo Bridge and part of London's artsy South Bank, MoMI hardly enjoys the most picturesque of locations (witness 'Four Weddings and a Funeral'). But you don't have to be a film connoisseur (or indeed any kind of connoisseur) to follow MoMI's jaunt down 'the yellow brick road' of film and television history. The museum advises

MUSEUMS - CENTRAL

False Maria from Fritz Lang's Metropolis, The Museum of the Moving Image

visitors to allow 2 hours for a visit – but if in doubt about time, look out for the handy 'pacing the museum' wall charts which are dotted around the galleries.

Packed with photographic and film equipment (from primitive to ultra-sophisticated), memorabilia and costume, MoMI is also staffed by a lively team of actor-guides in period costumes. Marked by their knowledge of exhibits and ability to stay in character, these guides are apparently one of the most popular features of museum and, love'em or loathe'em, they certainly liven up a visit. Climb aboard the Agitprop train where a Russian revolutionary guides you through the radical filmography of Eisenstein and Pudovkin, or visit a Hollywood casting office for a salacious trawl through the goldfish bowl world of the film star.

A look at the golden years of the silver screen, the Sound Stage is an amalgam of pirate galleon and Wild West saloon – and if you think this is confusing, just wait until you've had a look at 'Precious Images', a six minute sprint through 500 movies. The Sound Stage is also home to some of the museum's best exhibits: Boris Karloff's stand-in for 'Frankenstein', Fred'n'Ginger costumes and Marilyn Monroe's black shimmy dress from 'Some Like it Hot'. The myriad departments which make up the movie machine are also explored: tap on the scriptwriter's typewriter to hear some of best ever lines in the movies. It's a pity Hollywood's literary talents weren't around to edit some of the labels in the museum though – a few could do with a bit of updating and some exhibits are beginning to look a bit frayed around the edges too.

Technical exhibits explain how colour, special effects and sound came to be integral to filmmaking – although the concept of sound being recorded as a photographic image is still a tricky one to grasp. The animation gallery should appeal particularly to children – and scientifically-challenged adults. Original drawings from a plethora of cartoons are displayed here and a professional animator is on hand to show visitors how to make their own drawings move – although if 'Gertie the Dinosaur' (a three minute short comprising 3,000 individual drawings) is anything to go by, you may prefer to simply watch the Animator in Residence at work in the studio.

Like many of London's museums, MoMI can't resist playing the nostalgia card – its display of the lost 'picture palaces' which preceded today's multiplex mediocrities should have a few cinema-goers reaching for their hankies. In the same way, the television galleries will strike a chord with couch potatoes of all ages – children's programmes and adverts seem particularly potent memory joggers. The last gallery brings the visitor into the not very charismatic world of video and satellite broadcasting, although special effects gizmos let visitors fly like Superman over the streets of London and read the news on television.

MoMI's yellow brick road finally emerges through the museum exit to deposit the visitor – a cynical touch this – in the 'Moving Image Store'. Replete with an enticing array of merchandise, the 'store' is an ideal location for a parent-child battle of the will. Tempers can be restored over a drink and a snack at the new and long-awaited café at the National Film Theatre.

The Museum of the Order of St John

- 🏠 *St John's Gate, St John's Lane EC1*
- 📞 *0171 253 6644*
- 🚌 *Transport: Farringdon LU*
- 🕐 *Mon-Fri 10.00-17.00, Sat 10.00-16.00 (Guided tours Tues, Fri, Sat 11.00 and 14.30)*
- 🏵 *Admission free (donations accepted for tours)*
- 🛍 *Shop*
- ♿ *Wheelchair access (museum only)*

A sturdy C16th gatehouse is the picturesque setting for this museum, which tells the story of the Order of St John from its foundation in the Middle Ages to its present day form: the St John Ambulance. Warlike defender of the faith on one hand, merciful providers for the poor and sick on the other, the role of the original Order seems a tad contradictory. One room contains assorted bits of armour, including a rare chain mail outfit and coins minted by the crusaders, while elsewhere the exhibits include colourful majolica pharmacy jars and a scale model of the Order's ophthalmic hospital in Jerusalem.

The guided tours take about 1¼ hours and are well worthwhile, giving access to the church and parts of the gatehouse not normally open to the public. As well as soaking up the archaic atmosphere, visitors can admire portraits of the Order's top brass, fine silverware and books. There are also some interesting pieces of Maltese furniture (a remnant of the order's long association with the island), one particularly intricate cabinet contains 50 secret compartments. The gatehouse still boasts its original wooden spiral staircase and, a short distance away, the C12th crypt in the Order's church is home to a beautiful carved alabaster effigy of a Spanish knight. Run by the St John Ambulance, the shop sells a range of first aid products and uniforms along with a selection of more conventional souvenirs.

Museums of the Royal College of Surgeons of England

(The Hunterian Museum, Odontological Museum, Wellcome Museums of Pathology and Anatomy)

- 🏠 *35-43 Lincoln's Inn Fields, WC2*
- 📞 *0171 973 2190*
- 🚌 *Transport: Holborn LU*
- 🕐 *Mon-Fri 10.00-17.00 (Wellcome Museums by appointment only)*
- 🏵 *Admission free*
- 🛍 *Shop*
- ♿ *Wheelchair access by arrangement*

Packed with case upon glass case of anatomical and pathological specimens, human and otherwise, the Hunterian Museum and its fellows at the RCS are specialist medical museums.

Many of the preparations are C18th originals belonging to John Hunter whose research into bone growth, regeneration and reproduction paved the way for modern scientific surgery. Not without their own macabre beauty, the specimen jars contain all sorts of innards and outards suspended in sepulchral solutions – the section on digestion features the head of a King Vulture, an elephant's molar and the alimentary canal of a sea cucumber. After these, it's almost a relief to look at the skeletons which feature the 7ft 10inch frame of 'the Irish Giant' Charles Byrne, several criminals and a solitaire (an equally defunct relative of the dodo). Animal paintings by George Stubbs and Jacques-Laurent Agasse and busts of medical men are also among the exhibits.

The toothsome treasures of the odontological museum next door include Anglo-Saxon skulls, a dinosaur fang and Queen Caroline's dentures – it's interesting, if sad, to see that animals suffer from the same dental problems as humans. There are further medical exhibits at the Wellcome Museums which can be visited only by appointment.

MUSEUMS - CENTRAL

33

The Museum of the Royal Pharmaceutical Society

⌖ *1 Lambeth High Street, SE1*
☏ *0171 735 9141*
🚌 *Transport: Vauxhall LU, Lambeth North LU, Waterloo LU*
🕘 *Mon-Fri 9.00-13.00, 14.00-17.00 (for non-members of RPSGB visits are by guided tour, by prior appointment)*
🎟 *Admission free*
♿ *Limited wheelchair access*

This specialist museum traces the long history of medicinal drugs and their use. Its collection is particularly strong on community and retail pharmacy from C17th onwards and among the pharmaceutical paraphernalia are 'delftware' apothecary jars, dispensing equipment, advertisements for patent medicines and 'druggists' sundries'. Guided tours last approximately 1 hour; there are no catering facilities on site but the Museum of Garden History (p.28) is just over the road and has an excellent café.

The Museum of St Bartholomew's Hospital

⌖ *West Smithfield, EC1*
☏ *0171 601 8033/8152*
🚌 *Transport: Farringdon LU, St Paul's LU, Barbican LU*
🕘 *Tues-Fri 10.00-16.00*
🎟 *Admission free*
📦 *Shop*

Founded in 1123, St Bart's is what you might call well-established. Its small museum reflects the Hospital's antiquity with documents dating from C12th (including one signed by Henry VIII), works of arts, and surgical equipment. There is a small museum shop and visitors can glimpse two uncharacteristically grandiose paintings by William Hogarth (see p.76) on the staircase leading to the Hospital's Great Hall.

The National Postal Museum

⌖ *King Edward Building, Kind Edward St, EC1*
☏ *0171 600 8914*
🚌 *Transport: St Paul's LU, Barbican LU*
🕘 *Mon-Fri 9.30-16.30*
🎟 *Admission free*
📦 *Shop*

If you don't know a pillar box from a Penny Black you soon will at the NPM. Recently refurbished and situated in the imposing former London Chief Post Office, the museum is a philatelist's heaven but should appeal to anyone who's ever enjoyed getting a letter.

On the ground floor, a well-presented exhibition 'Post Haste!' tells how the Post Office has delivered the mail over the centuries. It's an engaging story – pirates, snow storms and escaped lionesses have all delayed the mail, not to mention five-wheeled bicycles. More conventional postal vehicles on display range from a 1930's Morris delivery van to a wagon from the Post Office's own underground railway. Historic street furniture includes pillar boxes cast for the reign of Edward VIII and an example of the so-called 'anonymous' box (the designers forgot to put the Royal Cipher on). Technophiles can admire 'Elsie', a magnificent pea-green sorting machine dating from the 1950's.

Naturally, there are stamps galore too – housed in neat pull out display cases and arranged thematically (cats, flowers etc.), by British monarch and by country. Museum staff are friendly and happy to point out unusual items like the snail-savaged letter from Cornwall (marked 'stamp eaten by snails'). The museum's extensive holdings also include the childhood stamp album of the late Freddie Mercury – available by appointment.

Philatelic books and a range of rather pricey 'collectable' models are available from the museum shop, along with smaller, more affordable souvenirs.

The Herb Garret

The Old Operating Theatre Museum and Herb Garret

- 🖼 *9a, St Thomas' Street, SE1*
- ☎ *0171 955 4791*
- 🚌 *Transport: London Bridge LU*
- ⏰ *Tues-Sun 10.00-16.00*
  (and some Mondays, ring first)
- 🏷 *Admission £2.90 (adults), £2.00 (concessions), £1.50 (children), £7.25 (families)*
- 🛍 *Shop*

Located in the garret of St Thomas' Church, the Old Operating Theatre is perhaps London's most atmospheric museum, as well as one of its most inaccessible. A rickety wooden spiral staircase leads up to the displays, a precipitous climb unsuitable for those with restricted mobility but well worth the effort for those who can make it.

The operating theatre (the oldest in the country) is the centrepiece of the museum and a grisly remnant of pre-anaesthetic and antiseptic surgery it is

too. A semi-circular arena overlooked by raised tiers with leaning rails (from where medical students watched the bloody proceedings), it was not called a theatre for nothing – although the scarred wooden operating table looks better suited to the kitchen than the hospital.

Festooned with dried herbs hanging from the wooden eaves, the adjacent Apocathary's Garret is only marginally less gruesome. Pickled human specimens are also displayed here, along with some worryingly indelicate medical instruments like amputation kits and obstetrics tools with off-putting names like 'blunt hook and crochet' and 'Smellies petrorator'. Standing as it does on the site of the original St Thomas' Hospital, the museum also has displays on medieval monastic health care, Florence Nightingale (on whose advice the Hospital moved to Lambeth) and even John Keats, who studied medicine at Guy's hospital before becoming a full time poet.

The Percival David Foundation of Chinese Art

- 53 Gordon Square, WC1
- 0171 387 3909
- Transport: Russell Square LU, Goodge Street LU, Euston Square LU
- Mon-Fri 10.30-17.00
- Admission free (donations appreciated)
- Shop

Finding this sumptuous collection of Chinese ceramics in the depths of London's student heartland was a treat. Spanning the C10th-C18th, the collection is extensive but of the highest calibre: a breathtaking showcase of the potter's art.

Of particular note are stonewares from the Song and Yuan dynasties which include pieces of Ru ware – the rarest of all Chinese ceramics. Highly decorated blue and white porcelain and polychrome pottery is also well represented. Despite their antiquity, the clean lines and often vibrant colours of many of these pieces wouldn't look out of place in some of Tottenham Courts Road's trendier lifestyle stores. Although there isn't much in the way of information for the lay person, the displays are enough of a visual feast for it not to matter too much.

For committed pot-heads – or for those who want to learn more about Chinese ceramics – the guide to the collection is a good investment at £9.95.

Petrie Museum of Egyptian Archaeology

- University College London, Gower Street, WC1
- 0171 5042884
- Transport: Euston Square LU, Russell Square, LU, Goodge Street LU, Euston LU
- Mon-Fri 10.00-17.00 (closed 12.00-13.15)
- Admission free
- Sales point

Founded by the father of Egyptian archaeology, W.M.F. Petrie, and recently voted one of London's top ten little-known museums, the Petrie is a treasure trove for Egyptophiles. With its huge collection of artifacts dating from Pre-dynastic times to the Roman era, it's the ideal place to get acquainted with the everyday life of ancient Egyptians and the cultural developments of one of the world's greatest civilizations. The well-stocked sales point carries a good selection of Egyptology titles for both adults and children, sterling silver jewellery by Antoinette Wheeldon (from £13-£22) and reasonably priced replica sculptures such as the 'haematite hippopotamus-head weight' for £8.50.

Pollock's Toy Museum

- 1 Scala Street, W1
- 0171 636 3452
- Transport: Goodge Street LU
- Mon-Sat 10.00-17.00
- Admission £2.50 (adults), £1.00 (under 18's)
- Shop

Set in two adjoining houses and comprising just six small rooms, this dinky museum is packed to the rafters with toys, games and pastimes. Even the narrow, winding staircases double up as display areas, covering topics as diverse as 'penny dreadfuls' and educational board games. With every available nook pressed into

Mummy Portrait, The Petrie Museum

service, many exhibits are at child height (although as with other toy museums in London, (see p.48 & p.77) adults will have as much fun looking round as kids).

There's an incredible range of toys on show: from puppets to puzzles, tin toys to Tyrolean carved animals, from Victorian wax dolls to space toys to the short-lived 'Falklands War Game'. An endearing group of veteran teddy bears live under the eaves in room 2 and literary types should look out for novelist E.M. Forster's childhood tin soldiers in the boy's den.

Named in honour of toy theatre-maker Benjamin Pollock, the museum devotes a whole room to the 'Juvenile Drama' – colourful paper and cardboard confections to stir the hearts and mind of young thesps. Ready-to-assemble theatres are sold in the shop, which also stocks a selection of old fashioned toys like jack-in-the-boxes and top quality soft toys.

Prince Henry's Room
- *17 Fleet Street, EC4*
- *0181 294 1158*
- *Transport: Temple LU*
- *Mon-Sat 11.00-14.00*
- *Admission free*

Built in 1610 as an office for King James's eldest son, this funny little room has in its time been a tavern and a waxworks. It now houses a rather thin collection of artifacts relating to diarist Samuel Pepys but it's worth a peek if only for the fine Jacobean plaster ceiling, wood panelling and quaint leaded light windows overlooking the bustle of Fleet Street.

Royal College of Obstretricians & Gynaecologists
- *27 Sussex Place, Regent's Park, NW1*
- *0171 262 5425*
- *Transport: Baker Street LU*
- *Mon-Fri 10.00-17.00 (by appointment)*
- *Admission Free*
- *Wheelchair access*

This specialist museum of medical instruments is open only to historians and those in the medical profession.

Royal College of Physicians
- *11 St Andrew's Place, NW1*
- *0171 935 1174*
- *Transport: Regent's Park LU, Great Portland Street LU*
- *Mon-Fri 10.00-17.00*
- *Admission free by appointment only*
- *Wheelchair access*

Portraits of notable physicians past and present can be examined here – from paintings of Sir Hans Sloane and John Radcliffe to a sculpture of Sir Raymond Hoffenberg by Dame Elizabeth Frink. For those with a particular interest in medical history.

MUSEUMS - CENTRAL

MUSEUMS - CENTRAL

Royal Fusiliers Museum

- HM Tower of London, EC3
- 0171 480 6082
- Transport: Tower Hill
- Daily 9.30-17.15
- Admission 50p in addition to entrance fee to HM Tower of London
- Shop

Having just paid a hefty entrance fee to get into the Tower, visitors may balk at having to shell out extra to look around this small regimental museum. However, for your 50p you get a coherent, concise account of the Fusiliers' history from 1685 right up to the Gulf War and beyond, and a pretty good idea of what life was like for soldiers in the past. Artifacts range from the innocuous (regimental egg cups) to the deadly (some of the shot and shell fired over No Man's Land in WWI).

St Bride's Crypt

- St Bride's Church, Fleet Street, EC4
- 0171 353 1301
- Transport: Blackfriars LU
- Daily 9.00-17.00
- Admission free

From the top of its wedding cake spire to the depths of its crypt, St Bride's is steeped in history. Badly bombed in WWII, Christopher Wren's church (the eighth on the site) was restored to its former glory – but not before excavations revealed the site's previously unknown Roman origins. Some of these and later archaeological finds are displayed in the small museum in the crypt: clay pots and pipes, coins and fire-distorted fragments of the old church's bells. Although the newspaper offices have decamped downriver, St Brides still remains the parish church for the industry once known collectively as 'Fleet Street' and the crypt museum also explores the church's connections with the trade – from Caxton to the demise of 'Ink Street'.

The Salvation Army Heritage Centre

- 117-121 Judd Street, WC1
- 0171 387 1656
- Transport: King's Cross LU, Euston LU
- Mon-Fri 9.30-15.30, Sat 9.30-12.30
- Admission free
- Shop
- Wheelchair access

All you ever wanted to know about the Salvation Army and more. This permanent exhibition tells how William Booth was inspired to help the poor and homeless and how the Sally-Am survived persecution to grow into an international organisation. The display cases are rather densely packed with memorabilia – badges, bonnets, tambourines and items like the 'Salvation Soldier's Song Book' – but there's a free audio guide to help visitors navigate their way around.

Shakespeare's Globe

- New Globe Walk, SE1
- 0171 902 1500
- Transport: London Bridge LU, Cannon Street LU, Mansion House LU
- Mon-Sun Individuals: May-Sept 9.00-12.15 and 14.00-16.00, Oct-April 10.00-17.00; Groups: May-Sept 9.00-12.30, Oct-April 10.00-17.00
- Admission £5 (adults), £4 (concessions), £3 (children)
- Shop,
- Café and Restaurant
- Wheelchair access

A permanent exhibition devoted to Shakespeare and his contemporaries is due to open here in 1999. In the meantime, while work continues on the International Shakespeare Globe Centre, a temporary exhibition introduces visitors to the Bard's 'Wooden O'. A guided tour is included in the price of entrance ticket – although it's more of a talk than a tour.

The Sherlock Holmes Museum

- 221b Baker Street, NW1
- 0171 935 8866
- Transport: Baker Street LU
- Daily 9.30-18.00
- Admission £5 (adults), £3 (under 16s)
- Shop and restaurant

A museum dedicated to a fictional character does seem to stretch the definition of what a museum is and what its purpose should be. This one aims to show visitors exactly how the great detective and his sidekick Watson would have lived in their C19th lodgings – although as far as I recall the intrepid duo made do without an in-house souvenir shop and restaurant.

Smythson

- 40 New Bond Street, W1
- 0171 629 8558
- Transport: Bond Street LU
- Mon-Fri 9.30-17.30, Sat 10.00-17.30
- Admission Free
- Wheelchair Access

Frank Smythson Limited has been catering for the smart set's stationery needs since 1887 and for many this Mayfair emporium is still the last word in leather bound luxury and pukka paper. Items from the company's archive are displayed in the small museum at the back of the shop: monogrammed paper, photograph albums, engraved wedding invitations and calling cards, monogrammed seals and luscious leather samples reflecting the tastes of clients who included maharajahs and royals. Even the shell-encrusted grotto which houses the display is impeccably well connected, having been designed by the architect who remodelled Downing Street.

Shakespeare's Globe Theatre

MUSEUMS - CENTRAL

Sir John Soane's Museum

📧 *13 Lincoln's Inn Fields, WC2*
📞 *0171 430 0175 (information line)*
📞 *0171 405 2107 (administration)*
🚌 *Transport: Holborn LU*
🕐 *Tues-Sat 10.00-17.00,*
   first Tuesday of month 18.00-21.00
💰 *Admission free*
🛍 *Shop*

Sir John Soane was the most original architect of his day. Luckily for us, his house was established as a museum during his lifetime and today remains much as it did when he died – a wonderfully dotty creation. The labyrinth of rooms, each one more fantastical than the last, is a testament to Soane's vision. Clearly he was a stranger to today's mania for minimalism – every available nook is home to some treasure or other. When they're not made of stained glass or smothered with mirrors, walls are encrusted with fragments of antique marble statuary. The Dome & Colonnade features larger works like a cast of the Apollo Belvedere – an art historical icon despite the strategically placed fig leaf – and a bust of Soane himself looking uncannily like Julius Caesar.

Ingenious hinged-screen walls in the Picture Room allow over 100 paintings to be displayed in this modest space – amongst them Hogarth's biting political satire 'The Election' and his scathing look at contemporary morals 'The Rake's Progress'. Gothic morbidity is the order of the day in the basement which comes complete with a skeleton in the closet, monk's cell, Pharaonic sarcophagus and a hoard of Roman cinerary urns. After all these excesses, the upstairs Drawing Room seems the model of good taste.

A guided lecture tour takes place every Saturday at 2.30pm to bring order to the apparent chaos. Tickets cost £3 and are limited so arrive early to ensure a place.

The Soane's Museum

Spencer House

📧 *27 St James's Place, W1*
📞 *0171 499 8620*
🚌 *Transport: Green Park LU*
🕐 *Sun 10.30-17.50 (last tour 16.45; tours last approx 1 hour)*
💰 *Admission £6 (adults), £5 (concessions)*
♿ *Wheelchair Access*

This private palace was originally built for the 1st Earl Spencer, an C18th ancestor of Diana, Princess of Wales. Thanks to a 10 year restoration programe, the building has regained its opulent neoclassical appearance. Its swanky state rooms include the Palm Room – a positive jungle of gilded fronds and foliage – and the Painted Room, designed by James 'Athenian' Stuart and now reunited at last with the furniture he designed for it. Paintings on loan from the Royal Collection are among the art works on display. Access is by guided tour only.

The Theatre Museum

- 🖳 *1e Tavistock Street, WC2*
- 🕿 *0171 836 7891*
- 🚌 *Transport: Covent Garden LU*
- 🕐 *Tues-Sun: 11.00-19.00*
- 💰 *Admission £3.50 (adults),*
  £2.00 (concessions)
- 🛍 *Shop*
- ♿ *Wheelchair access*

Set in the heart of London's Luvvie-land, this is the National Museum of the Performing Arts. A flamboyant display of costumes in the foyer makes an eye-catching curtain raiser while in the museum itself celeb-spotters should enjoy the museum's wall of fame featuring the multicoloured hand prints of luminaries like Dame Peggy Ashcroft and Sir John Gielgud.

Charting the history of the British theatre from the age of Shakespeare to the present day, the subterranean main gallery is rather more sedate and encumbered by tiny, difficult to read labels. Impressive though they may be to connoisseurs, 400 years' worth of playbills, posters, stage sets, props, paintings and photos trapped behind glass can only go so far in conjuring up the buzz of live theatre. Some of the more gripping exhibits however, include hand-painted costumes from Nijinsky's riot-provoking production of 'The Rites of Spring' and memorabilia of assorted thesps, including one of Noel Coward's signature silk dressing gowns.

But the play's the thing here and the museum really shines with 'The Wind in the Willows – from page to stage', a display which takes the visitor backstage to reveal how a novel is transformed into an award-winning theatre production. Everyone from the actors to the lowliest of backstage johnnies is given an equal share of the limelight and stage struck of all ages can watch Toad, Ratty and Co. in rehearsal

Costume workshops at the Theatre Museum

(on video), eavesdrop on the Deputy Stage Manager during a performance, peer at the prompt book and make sure everthing's in place on the all important props table.

Another fun exhibition, 'Slap!' celebrates the ever-evolving art of stage make-up and, on a more participatory note, features popular free demonstrations (held throughout the day). The 'Recording Performance' exhibition introduces the TM's recently established National Video Archive of Stage Performance and also includes sound recordings – your chance to compare Gielgud's 1948 Hamlet with Kenneth Branagh's more recent interpretation, and hear Henry Irving's 1888 performance as Richard III.

Costume workshops and guided tours are also available and the museum runs a regular programme of events and talks.

The View east from Walkway, The Tower Bridge Experience

The Tower Bridge Experience

- 🖭 *Tower Bridge, SE1*
- 📞 *0171 403 3761*
- 📞 *0171 378 1928 (recorded information)*
- 🚌 *Transport: Tower Hill LU,
  London Bridge LU*
- 🕐 *Daily April-Oct 10.00-18.30,
  Nov-Mar 9.30- 18.00
  (last entry 1¼ hours before closing)*
- 💷 *Admission £5.95 (adults), £3.95 (children,
  OAP's), £14.95 (families)*
- 📦 *Shop*
- ♿ *Wheelchair access*

A triumph of Victorian civil engineering, Tower Bridge is one of London's most instantly recognisable landmarks. For those not content with admiring its Gothic silhouette from a distance, this imaginative tour around the bridge's innards should be just the thing. Characters from the bridge's past – spookily brought to life by some ultra realistic animatronics – act as other worldly guides, narrating the hows, whys and wherefores of this once controversial structure. However the C20th century wizardry is all but eclipsed by the Victorian technology on show in the Engine Rooms. Two massive steam engine pumps which once powered the famous drawbridge over the Thames are accompanied by equally gargantuan toolkits and there's what looks suspiciously like a school dinner gong on display in the engineer's gallery.

Taking in both North and South Towers, the 'Experience' also provides access to the two glassed-in walkways which link them. The spectacular views up and down river more than repay the climb up several staircases to reach them (a lift is available for disabled visitors) and there are even little camera windows so visitors can get that perfect shot of St Paul's. If it's 3-D souvenirs you're after, a spectacularly tiny model of the bridge comes in at just under a fiver at the giftshop.

Tower Hill Pageant

- 🖭 *Tower Hill, EC3*
- 📞 *0171 709 0081*
- 🚌 *Transport: Tower Hill LU*
- 🕐 *Daily 9.30-17.30 (Easter-October),
  9.30-16.30 (November-March)*
- 💷 *Admission £6.95 (adults), £4.95
  (children/concessions), £15.95 (families)*
- 📦 *Shop*
- 🍽 *Cafés*
- ♿ *Wheelchair access (telephone in advance)*

Don't be put off by the tourist packaging of this attraction. The Pageant's 'time ride' through 2000 years of London's history may sound tacky, but it's actually good fun and genuinely informative.

Taking the concept of 'armchair history' to its logical conclusion, the time cars haul visitors past successive snap shots of the City's past: a rough and ready Saxon market, Viking invaders, a Tudor merchant ship and so on right up to the present day. Commentaries are available in a variety of languages – although how the 'gor' blimey' Mockney of the English version translates into Japanese I would love to know.

Budding archaeologists should enjoy rooting around the waterfront finds which provide the real meat of the Pageant. Old Father Thames' receding waterline has left behind rich pickings for the excavators: artifacts here include original Roman and Medieval timber quays – there is also a reconstruction of a Roman ship found at Blackfriars. Unlike many museums this one actually explains how archaeologists work and visitors can study fragments of pottery under the microscope to discover how such tiny objects are dated. Other objects include a skeleton from Britain's only known plague cemetery and Europe's oldest pair of specs, while a display of medieval tourist tat literally rubbishes our idea that every archaeological find must be a priceless work of art.

MUSEUMS - CENTRAL

The Tower of London

⌖ *Tower Hill, EC3*

☏ *0171 709 0765*

🚌 *Transport: Tower Hill LU*

🕐 *Mon-Sat 9.00-18.00, Sun 10.00-18.00*

🎟 *Admission £9.00 (adults), £6.80 (concessions), £5.90 (children), £26.90 (families) Tickets also available from most underground stations*

❧ *Shop*

☕ *Cafés*

♿ *Some wheelchair access*

London's tourist trail just wouldn't be complete without the Tower. Saturated with tradition, history and the special brand of arcane ceremony that Britain does so well, the Tower attracts a staggering 2.5 million visitors a year. Perhaps best known as a royal prison, several walls still bear the inscriptions carved by 'guests' and the scaffold site on Tower Green – scene of Anne Boleyn's execution – is commemorated with a

Chief Yeoman Warder, The Tower of London

plaque. (Access to many of the towers is via narrow, spiral staircases and prams and pushchairs must be left outside buildings). The traditional guardians of the Tower, the Beefeaters, double up as guides and lead regular free tours and talks, giving plenty of coverage to the bloodier goings on. For those going it alone, the buildings are well labelled and free maps are available. An audio tour, 'Prisoners of the Tower' costs £1.50.

Now that the bulk of the Royal Armouries' arms and armour have been relocated to Leeds, and while the White Tower is being refurbished to make way for new displays, there's not much in the way of armour to be seen here. The new displays are scheduled to open in Summer 1998. Until then if you're really enamoured of armour and you don't fancy a trip up north, The Wallace Collection (p.112) has an excellent armoury (and it's free).

Metalwork of a different kind can be admired in the Jewel House where the coronation regalia of British monarchs makes for a dazzling display. The phrase conspicuous consumption could have been invented for the Crown Jewels: the Cullinan diamond in the Sovereign's Sceptre may not be as big as the Ritz but it isn't far off and is, in any case, the world's largest top quality cut diamond. Another hefty sparkler – the fabled Kor-i-Noor diamond – is the jewel in the Queen Mum's crown while older regalia includes the St Edward's Crown and the C12th Coronation spoon. For those not thoroughly versed in Royal ceremonials, footage of the coronation in 1953 introduces the displays but if you're still none the wiser the fully illustrated guide book comes in at £3.50.

With no less than four souvenir shops and its own on-site currency exchange, retail opportunities are never very far away at the Tower, but with adult entrance at over £8 a throw, visitors may feel their wallets have taken enough of a battering.

Twinings in the Strand

- 🏠 *216 Strand, WC2*
- 📞 *0171 353 3511*
- 📞 *01264 334 477 (group bookings)*
- 🚌 *Transport: Temple LU*
- 🕐 *Mon-Fri 9.30-16.30*
- 🎟 *Admission free*
- 📖 *Shop*

This museum – in reality a small room at the end of the shop – celebrates the lengthy history of this renowned tea and coffee merchants with intriguing memorabilia such as tea 'bricks' and the coffee house T.I.P. box – a reminder of days when customers paid a gratuity before ordering 'To Insure Promptness'. The 'museum' doubles up as a boardroom so it's not always open to the public and group visits are by appointment only.

Twinings in the Strand

University College Art Collection

- 🏠 *Strang Print Room, South Cloister, Main Building, UCL, Gower Street, WC1*
- 📞 *0171 387 7050 ext 2540*
- 🚌 *Transport: Euston LU, Warren St LU, Euston Square LU, Goodge Street LU*
- 🕐 *Wed-Fri 13.00-17.00 (during term time)*
- 🎟 *Admission Free*
- ♿ *Wheelchair Access*

Administered by the Strang Print Room, University College owns over 600 hundred paintings, 7,000 prints and drawings and some 150 sculptures. The Print Room itself is home to works by Old Masters such as Dürer, Cranach and Rembrandt and holds regular public exhibitions. The Slade collection traces the development of art education in England and includes early works by Stanley Spencer and Augustus John as well as C20th drawings from professors and students at the Slade School. The Reserve Collection may be viewed by appointment.

University College Geology Collections

- 🏠 *Room 4, South Wing, UCL, Gower Street, WC1*
- 📞 *0171 387 7050 (ext 7900)*
- 🚌 *Transport: Euston LU, Warren St LU, Euston Square LU, Goodge Street LU*
- 🕐 *Wed lunchtimes and other times by appointment*
- 🎟 *Admission Free*
- ♿ *Wheelchair access*

The aptly named Rock Room houses this collection containing 40,000 geological specimens from all over the world – from fossils to meteorites and minerals.

The Wellcome Trust

'Science for Life'; History of Medicine Gallery

🏠 *183 Euston Road, NW1*

🕐 *0171 611 7211 (recorded information)*

🕐 *0171 611 8888 (wheelchair access/facilities)*

🚌 *Transport: Euston LU, Euston Square LU, Warren Street LU*

🕐 *Mon-Fri 9.45-17.00, Sat 9.45-13.00*

🍽 *Admission free*

♿ *Wheelchair access*

Another of London's medically-minded attractions, the 'Science for Life' exhibition is also one of the most rewarding. With its snappy, award-winning design and genuinely interactive exhibits, it's a lot more fun than your average science lesson.

The invitation to 'explore the body' involves everything from getting to grips with intestines (actually an almost never ending piece of rubber hose) to testing your short term memory to examining diseased tissue under the microscope. Magnified one million times, a single human cell is here transformed into a walk-through area, taking visitors to the nucleus and bringing them face to face with a 'dangerous digester' en route.

On a practical note, an excellent computer game ('Laboratory Workbench') gives the visitor the chance to play at being a medical researcher gathering data and forming hypotheses. Knotty ethical issues are raised and the huge advances of this century placed alongside some medical mysteries yet to be cracked (each one accompanied by an impressively up to date file of newspaper cuttings). A multimedia resource area is also available.

Enormously popular since its opening in 1993, 'Science for Life' will be relocated to Manchester Museum in Spring/Summer 1999. A full programme of events will however be maintained at the Euston Road site and the History of Medicine gallery will continue to host temporary exhibitions.

The Wellcome Trust

Two 10 Gallery

🏠 *210 Euston Road, NW1*

🚌 *Transport: Euston LU, Euston Square LU, Warren Street LU*

🕐 *Mon-Fri 9.00-18.00*

The Wellcome Trust holds 3-4 temporary exhibitions about science and art at this venue each year. Past shows have included 'The Art of Medicine' and 'Saving bodies, saving souls: hospitals in history'.

Westminster Abbey Museum

🏠 *Westminster Abbey, SW1*

🕐 *0171 233 0019*

🚌 *Transport: St James Park LU*

🕐 *Daily 10.30-16.00*

🍽 *Admission £2.50 (adults), £1.90 (concessions), £1.30 (children), English Heritage Members free*

🛍 *Shop*

☕ *Coffee Stall*

Compared to the worldly hubbub of the Abbey, this museum (located in an ancient vaulted undercroft) is almost church-like in its tranquillity. Its collection of funeral effigies are certainly bizarre enough to reduce the most garrulous tourist to silence. Compelling viewing, the macabre waxwork portraits include those of Edward III, Elizabeth I, and Charles II (sporting his garter robes). Lord Nelson's effigy joins this royal company and was much admired by his contemporaries (although Nelson himself was buried at St Paul's Cathedral, see p.17). Other artifacts on display include a recycled Roman sarcophagus and decidedly unconvincing replica set of the crown jewels used for coronation rehearsals (the real McCoy can be seen at the Tower of London, p.44).

The admission price includes entry to the historic Pyx Chamber with its treasury of church plate, and the medieval Chapter House.

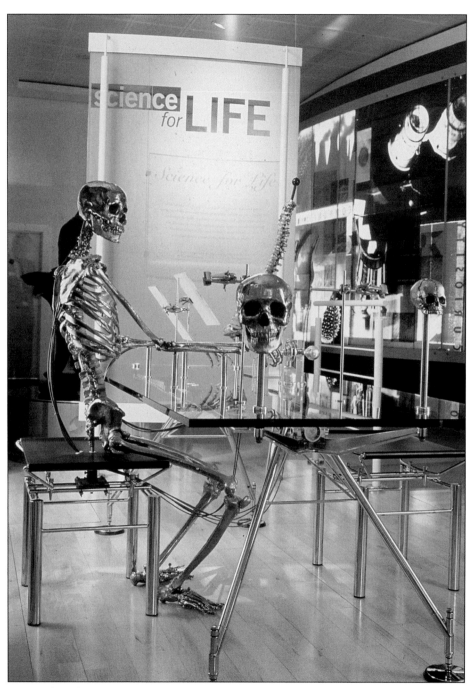

Science for Life, The Wellcome Trust

MUSEUMS - EAST

EAST

Bethnal Green Museum of Childhood

- 🏢 *Cambridge Heath Road, E2*
- 📞 *0181 980 2415 (recorded information)*
- 🚌 *Transport: Bethnal Green LU*
- 🕐 *Mon-Thur, Sat 10.00-17.50,*
  Sun 14.30-17.50
- ♨ *Admission free*
- 🏷 *Shop*
- 🍵 *Café*
- ♿ *Wheelchair access (by advance arrangement)*

You don't have to have a sprog in tow to enjoy this museum. If anything, its vast hoard of toys from different eras and countries makes it just as appealing for misty-eyed adults. With a fine collection of children's clothes and equipment like potties and prams, the museum also illustrates the social history of childhood – from birth to the hormone-crazed days of adolescence – but few will be able to resist embarking on a voyage to rediscover the toys and games of their youth.

Among the more traditional toys visitors can admire are teddy bears, battalions of soldiers (Action Man gets his own display), rocking horses, trainsets and countless dolls. An authentic Punch and Judy booth should stir those seaside memories and there's also a big display of puppets from around the world. Pride of place though must go to the dolls houses, executed in every possible permutation of architectural style and degree of grandeur: from the opulence of '3 Devonshire Villas' to the Tudorbethan cosiness of 'Mrs Gupta's house' – enough to make any child (or estate agent) go weak at the knees.

As you might expect, the museum is very child-friendly. The airy Victorian galleries are spacious and well laid out, and at floor level throughout a sequence of toy boxes from 1780-1990 encourage kids to lift the lid on history. The toilets are equipped for nappy-changing and there's a play area in the café to keep youngsters amused while their elders chow down (those coping with fractious offspring will be pleased to learn that the café is licensed).

Doll's House c1890, Bethnal Green Museum of Childhood

48

The Regency Room, The Geffrye Museum

East Ham Nature Reserve

⊡ *Norman Road, E6*
🕓 *0181 470 4525*
🚌 *Transport: East Ham LU*
🕐 *Summer: Tues-Fri 10.00-17.00, Sat-Sun 14.00-17.00; Winter: Tues-Fri 10.00-16.00, Sat-Sun 13.00-16.00*
📖 *Admission Free*
📚 *Shop*
♿ *Wheelchair Access*

London's largest churchyard is home to this nature reserve, which is alive with wild plants, foxes, kestrels and lizards. Local history and wildlife displays can be tracked down in the visitor centre while the small shop provides an ideal habitat for souvenir-hunters.

The Geffrye Museum

⊡ *Kingsland Road, E2*
🕓 *0171 739 9893*
🚌 *Transport: Old Street LU (then 243 bus); Liverpool Street LU (then 22a, 22b or 149)*
🕐 *Tues-Sat 10.00-17.00, Sun and Bank Holiday Mondays 14.00-17.00*
📖 *Admission Free*
📚 *Shop*
☕ *Coffee bar*
♿ *Wheelchair access*

Set in C18th almshouses and one of London's more charismatic museums, the Geffrye offers visitors a voyeuristic treat by inviting them to go 'through the keyhole'. From the oak panelled simplicity of the C17th room to the cool elegance of the early Georgian room and the oppressive clutter of the Victorian parlour to jazzy art deco and post-war utility, the museum's series of fully-furnished period rooms presents the ever mutating face of English interior decoration. A kind of walk-through, 3-D source book of past taste, it's just as revealing about the way we live now as it is about domestic history. Activities and temporary exhibitions explore themes related to the rooms and their objects and the award-winning herb garden is an added attraction during the summer. Four new period rooms and a design centre will be the centrepiece of a new extension scheduled to open in November 1998.

Hackney Museum

⊡ *Parkside Library, Victoria Park Road E9*
🕓 *0181 986 6914*
(temporary location)

This local history museum will be operating a mobile service with temporary exhibitions being held at venues around the borough until the completion of its new building in summer 1999.

MUSEUMS - EAST

The London Gas Museum

▫️ *British Gas plc, Twelvetrees Crescent, E3*
📞 *0171 538 4982*
🚌 *Transport: Bromley-by-Bow LU*
🕐 *By appointment (telephone the Museum Administration Office on the above number, visits are arranged between 9.30-16.00)*
🎫 *Admission free*

Clock into this museum to discover the history of the capital's gas industry, from the C19th innovation of gas made from coal to modern manufacturing techniques. Boasting the world's largest collection of gas appliances, it's more than just a glorified showroom – video displays, working models and period rooms all play a part in telling the story of gas power in London.

Manor Park Museum and Library

▫️ *Romford Road, E12*
📞 *0181 514 0274*
🚌 *Transport: Manor Park BR*
🕐 *Tues 10.00-17.00, Thurs 13.00-20.00, Fri-Sat 10.00-17.00*
🎫 *Admission Free*
🛍️ *Shop*
♿ *Wheelchair Access*

Changing exhibitions on local history themes.

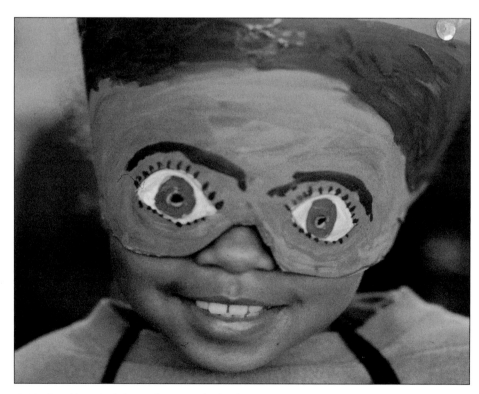

A Maskmaking Workshop, The Ragged School Museum

Metropolitan Police, Thames Division Museum

- 🏛 *Wapping Police Station, 99 Wapping High Street, E1*
- ☎ *0171 275 4421*
- 🚌 *Transport: Wapping LU*
- 🕐 *Open by appointment with the curator*
- 💰 *Admission free*

Part of a working police station, the museum tells the story of the Marine Police and the Thames Division with manuscripts from their early days, paintings, models and uniforms.

North Woolwich Old Station Museum

- 🏛 *Pier Road, E16*
- ☎ *0171 474 7244*
- 🚌 *Transport: North Woolwich BR*
- 🕐 *April-Sept Fri 14.00-17.00, Sat 10.00-17.00, Sun 14.00-17.00, Mon-Wed (school summer holidays and summer half-term only) 13.00-17.00*
- 💰 *Admission Free*
- 🛍 *Shop*
- ♿ *Wheelchair Access*

Railway engines, carriages, photographs and models from the now mythic 'golden age' of rail travel are the main attractions at this museum, housed in an old station. Displays about Newham's railway industry and workers strike a more local note, and on the first Sunday of summer months there is an engine in steam.

The Ragged School Museum

- 🏛 *46-50 Copperfield Road, E3*
- ☎ *0181 980 6405*
- 🚌 *Transport: Mile End LU*
- 🕐 *Wed, Thurs 10.00-17.00, first Sunday of the month 14.00-17.00*
- 💰 *Admission free (donations appreciated)*
- 🛍 *Shop*
- ☕ *Café*

Staffed by enthusiastic, friendly volunteers and set in an old canalside warehouse, this is a charismatic little museum. The site of London's largest Ragged (free) School, the museum focuses on the work of Dr Barnardo and education in London but its displays also explore the often harsh lives endured by East Enders in the last century, and the early years of this one. Guided tours are available for adult groups and as many of the volunteers are locals, these help to bring the past to life in a memorable way.

Decked out in the cream and maroon livery specified by Dr Barnardo and furnished with wooden desks, slates, an abacus and 'butterfly' blackboard, the reconstructed 1896 schoolroom makes an atmospheric centre piece. Around 8,500 primary school children a year take part in the popular re-enacted 'Victorian' lessons held here. During the school holidays there's a lively programme of events for children, adults and families – workshops, treasure hunts and story-telling are some of the activities on offer. Temporary exhibitions supplement the permanent displays and the museum shop also stocks local history publications along with a small selection of traditional-style toys and games. Snacks and drinks are sold in the Towpath Café.

Royal London Hospital Archives and Museum

- ▣ *Whitechapel High Street, E1 1BB*
- ◑ *0171 377 7000, ext 3364*
- ▦ *Transport: Whitechapel LU*
- ◷ *Mon-Fri 10.00-16.30*
- ▨ *Admission free (donations welcome)*
- ▧ *Shop*
- ♿ *Wheelchair access*

Located in the crypt of the former Hospital Church, this museum has an interesting selection of historic documents, medical equipment and nurses' uniforms as well as original artworks by William Hogarth and Sir John Lavery. The displays recount the history of the hospital from its founding in 1740 and highlight some of the medical developments it has witnessed like X-ray and cardiology, and the work of pioneers like Frederick Treves and Edith Cavell. There's also a small display about the hospital's most famous resident Joseph Merrick (the 'Elephant Man'). Books and cards are sold at the shop, and a video facility is available to visitors.

The Little Chamber, Sutton House

Sutton House

- ▣ *2 and 4 Homerton High Street, E9*
- ◑ *0181 986 2264*
- ▦ *Transport: Hackney BR*
- ◷ *Feb-Nov Wed, Sun and BH Mon 11.30-17.30*
- ▨ *Admission £1.80, £4.50 (families)*
- ▧ *Shop*
- ▭ *Café*
- ♿ *Disabled access ground floor only*

Tudor houses aren't exactly ten a penny in the capital these days and Sutton House is a rare survivor. Although on the receiving end of later additions and alterations the house contains early details like original linenfold panelling and C17th wall paintings. Set in Hackney, London's most arty borough, the house also hosts changing shows of contemporary art and sculpture.

Vestry House Museum

- ▣ *Vestry Road, E17*
- ◑ *0181 509 1917*
- ▦ *Transport: Walthamstow Central LU*
- ◷ *Mon-Fri 10.00-13.00, 14.00-17.30; Sat 10.00-13.00, 14.00-17.00*
- ▨ *Admission free*
- ▧ *Shop*
- ♿ *Wheelchair access (ground floor only)*

An exploration of the history of Walthamstow and its people. Locally made produce on show ranges from tin plate toys to the Bremer car of 1894 – the first car to be built in London. The Victorian parlour in the 'Hearth and Home' gallery may be a reconstruction, but the police cell is the real thing and although built in 1840 still has its original privy intact. Some of the museum's many historic photographs of Waltham Forest are on display – the rest of the collection, together with the archives and local history library, can be viewed by appointment.

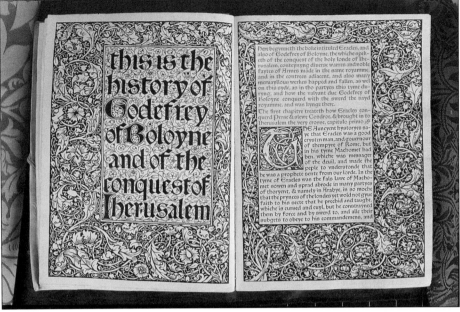

The William Morris Gallery

William Morris Gallery

- *Lloyd Park, Forest Road, E17*
- *0181 527 3782*
- *Transport: Walthamstow Central LU*
- *Tues-Sat (and first Sun of each month) 10.00-17.00 (closed 13.00-14.00)*
- *Admission free*
- *Shop*
- *Wheelchair access*

A visit to this museum is a life enhancing experience. Designer, writer and socialist, William Morris lived in this gracious Georgian house as a youth. Now its beautifully presented galleries illustrate the man's life and achievements and contain a comprehensive collection of richly decorative artifacts designed by Morris and his cronies.

Glowing stained glass panels, rustic furniture and textiles dense with flora and fauna encapsulate Morris's distinctive vision – among the treasures here is a copy of the Kelmscott Chaucer, the crowning achievement of the Kelmscott Press (see The William Morris Society p.91). Wallpaper and fabrics are shown alongside the labour intensive equipment used to make them in a vivid exploration of the processes behind the products and the horror Morris had of mass production. More personal exhibits include the canvas satchel he used for carrying Socialist literature and some his desk knick-knacks.

Upstairs is found Sir Frank Brangwyn's gift of paintings and drawings featuring works by Burne-Jones, Rossetti and Ford Madox Brown. Ironically though, it's Brangwyn's own vibrantly coloured, gutsy paintings which steal the show, making the Pre-Raphaelite imagery appear trite and mannered. A well-edited selection of Morris merchandise is available at the shop – the wipe down PVC apron (£8.50) a cunning commercial interpretation of his famous dictum 'have nothing in your houses that you do not know to be useful, or believe to be beautiful'.

MUSEUMS - NORTH

NORTH

Arsenal Football Club Museum

- ▢ *Arsenal Stadium, N5*
- ◔ *0171 704 1000*
- 🚌 *Transport: Arsenal LU*
- ◷ *Fri 9.30-16.00 (and other selected days)*
- 🏆 *Admission £2 (adults), £1 (children, OAPs)*
- ♿ *Wheelchair access*

Confirmed Arsenal fans may well be familiar with this museum (and know all there is to know about Arsenal FC) but for newcomers it's as good a place as any to be initiated. Sited in the North Bank of the Arsenal stadium, the museum recounts the club's eventful history from its poverty-stricken beginnings (when the team was so broke they couldn't afford their own shirts) to First Division glory days under Herbert Chapman's legendary 'hard but fair' management, and more recent triumphs and tribulations.

There's plenty of club memorabilia to keep Arsenal addicts of all ages happy – photographs, autographed match strips and trophies galore – but (for the complete novice at any rate) the museum's lively displays offer an invaluable insight into football in general. Kick off your visit with the film show 'The History of Arsenal' – presented by former Arsenal goalie Bob Wilson – and relive both the highs and the lows of the Gunners (it is a game of two halves).

Arsenal Football Club Museum

Bruce Castle Museum

- ▢ *Lordship Lane, N17*
- ◔ *0181 808 8772*
- 🚌 *Transport: Wood Green LU, then 243 bus*
- ◷ *Wed-Sun 13.00-17.00*
  (and Summer bank holidays)
- 🏆 *Admission free*
- ♿ *Wheelchair access (ground floor only)*

Although 'castle' is rather too generous a soubriquet, this historic building is one of only two Grade I listed buildings in Haringey. Once the manor house of Tottenham, Bruce Castle is now home to the borough's local history library and collections. Illustrating Haringey's evolution from rural idyll to sprawling suburb the displays include an original Roman pottery kiln as well as plenty of material relating to WWII. Postal history is the subject of the museum's most interesting display, reflecting the fact that Sir Rowland Hill, founder of the Penny Post, once lived at Bruce Castle. Early postmen's uniforms, letter-writing paraphernalia and even a highwayman's walking stick illustrate the origins of the modern postal service. A small assortment of telegraph and telephone equipment takes up the theme of communications and a collection of pillar boxes features a sky blue air mail model from the 1930's.

Burgh House

🖼 *New End Square, NW3*
📞 *0171 431 0144*
🚌 *Transport: Hampstead LU*
🕐 *Wed-Sun 12.00-17.00*
🏛 *Admission free*
🛍 *Shop*
☕ *Café*

Just off Hampstead's busy, bijoux High Street, this local history museum is a useful first port of call for those doing the cultural pilgrimage bit around this part of London. Housed in an elegant Queen Anne building, the museum shows how Hampstead has grown from sparsely-populated rural outpost to fashionable spa to affluent suburb. Hampstead has long since been a mecca for arty and literary types and exhibits at Burgh House include paintings by local artists and a display about Constable (who lived in the area for 15 years), and an endearing assortment of memorabilia. The book stall sells local history books and maps while in the basement the excellent Buttery serves good home-cooked food in cheery, unpretentious surroundings – a welcome refuge from Hampstead's serial shoppers and relentless café society.

Church Farmhouse Museum

🖼 *Greyhound Hill, Hendon, NW4*
📞 *0181 203 0130*
🚌 *Transport: Hendon Central LU*
🕐 *Mon-Thurs 10.00-12.30, 13.30-17.00,*
   Sat 10.00-13.00, 14.00-17.30,
   Sun 14.00-17.30
🏛 *Admission free*
🛍 *Shop*

Ten minutes walk and a world away from the teeming traffic of downtown Hendon, Church Farmhouse is a picturesque property dating from the reign of Charles II. Once the centre of a busy dairy and hay making enterprise, the farmhouse escaped post-war demolition by becoming Hendon's local history museum. A reconstructed Victorian laundry, kitchen and dining room are at the centre of the displays and the house itself retains the quirks of an historic building: low beamed ceilings, wonky wooden floors and narrow stairs. Well organised temporary exhibitions are held in the upstairs rooms – a recent one celebrated the life of George Pullman, inventor of a now outmoded concept: luxury train travel.

Fenton House

🖼 *Hampstead Grove, NW3*
📞 *0171 435 3471*
🚌 *Transport: Hampstead LU*
🕐 *Sat-Sun 14.00-17.00 (1-23 March);*
   Sat-Sun 11.00-17.30,
   Wed-Fri 14.00-17.30 (29 March-2 Nov)
🏛 *Admission £3.60, £9 (families)*

Known primarily for its collection of early keyboard instruments, this National Trust property also contains an interesting array of furniture, works of art and C18th porcelain. The orange and tangerine stripy wallpaper in the Dining Room forms a vivid backdrop to a group of no less delectable paintings by Sir William Nicholson, and elsewhere in the house there are displays of intricately-worked needlework pictures.

A late C17th merchant's house, Fenton House has clung onto a number of original features and is still surrounded by a large walled garden, making it a pleasant haven from Hampstead's bustling shops. Classical concerts are put on here throughout the year but if you're lucky you might hear a music student playing on one of the old spinets or harpsichords during your visit.

MUSEUMS - NORTH

55

The Freud Museum

🖾 *20 Maresfield Gardens, NW3*
📞 *0171 435 2002/5167*
🚌 *Transport: Finchley Road LU*
🕓 *Wed-Fri 12.00-17.00*
💳 *Admission £3 (adults), £1.50 (concessions), children under 12 free*
🛍 *Shop*
♿ *Wheelchair access to ground floor, help available for access to 1st floor*

A refugee escaping Nazi oppression, Sigmund Freud made this house his final home. Freud's study – an almost exact recreation of the one he vacated at his apartment in Vienna – remains as it did during his lifetime. Festooned with oriental rugs and lined with books, this room in particular offers a remarkable slice of fin de siècle Vienna. The centrepiece of the museum, the study is home to 'that' couch as well as to the many Egyptian, Greek, Roman and oriental antiquities Freud loved to collect. Preserved by a long period of burial, these objects from the past are worth seeing in their own right – for the founder of psychoanalysis they constituted the perfect analogy to his own archaeology of the subconscious.

On the landing hangs Salvador Dali's haunting portrait of the face that launched a thousand slips and upstairs, there's another couch – that belonging to Freud's psychoanalyst daughter Anna, who also lived at the house and whose pioneering work is also celebrated here. A video shows footage from the Freud family home movies and the shop is well stocked with titles covering the A-Z of psychoanalysis, along with gifts and jewellery inspired by Freudian theories.

Freud's psychoanalytic couch, The Freud Museum

The Grange Museum

- 🖺 *Neasden Roundabout, Neasden Lane, NW10*
- 🕾 *0181 452 8311*
- 🚌 *Transport: Neasden LU*
- 🕘 *Sept-May Mon-Fri 11.00-17.00, Sat 10.00-17.00, June-Aug Tues-Fri 11.00-17.00, Sat 10.00-17.00, Sun 14.00-17.00*
- 🎟 *Admission Free*
- ♿ *Wheelchair Access (ground floor only)*

A permanent local history display, topped up by a Victorian parlour, and Edwardian drapery. Each year the museum hosts a cultural exhibition.

Islington Museum

- 🖺 *268 Upper Street, N1*
- 🕾 *0171 354 9442 (gallery)*
- 🕾 *0171 477 3851 (museum office)*
- 🚌 *Transport: Highbury and Islington LU*
- 🕘 *Wed-Sat 11.00-17.00, Sun 14.00-16.00*
- 🎟 *Admission free*
- 👓 *Sales point*
- ♿ *Wheelchair access*

This museum in the heart of trendy N1 has a sturdy collection of objects with local significance, and acts as a local history resource centre as well as hosting a regular programme of exhibitions. (The museum will be re-locating down the street to the Town Hall at the end of June '98).

The Iveagh Bequest, Kenwood

- 🖺 *Hampstead Lane, NW3*
- 🕾 *0181 348 1286*
- 🚌 *Transport: Archway LU, Golders Green LU*
- 🕘 *Daily 10.00-18.00 (1 April-30 Sept), 10.00-16.00 (1 Oct-31 March)*
- 🎟 *Admission free*
- 👓 *Shops*
- 🖵 *Café*
- ♿ *Wheelchair access (ground floor only)*

With its elegant neo-classical architecture, beautiful picture collection and extensive

"The Guitar Player" by Vermeer

catering facilities and gift shops, Kenwood House is a favourite destination for many a Sunday afternoon walk on nearby Hampstead Heath.

Although its library is a good example of a lavishly-modelled interior by architect Robert Adam, Kenwood is not really one of those houses you visit for meticulously reconstructed period rooms. The Iveagh Bequest of paintings is the real draw and contains gems like Rembrandt's late, rather melancholy self portrait and Vermeer's 'The Guitar Player'. Works by British artists are plentiful and feature fine pieces by the stalwarts of C18th portraiture: Gainsborough, Reynolds and Romney. The much loved collection has recently been boosted by long term loans of early Renaissance paintings which include devotional works like Sandro Botticelli's 'Madonna and Child', and Hans Memling's 'Portrait of a Man in a Black Cap'.

The Jewish Museum

- *Raymond Burton House, 129-131 Albert Street, NW1*
- *0171 284 1997*
- *Transport: Camden Town LU*
- *Sun-Thurs 10.00-16.00 (closed Fridays and Jewish festivals)*
- *Admission £3.00 (adults), £1.50 (children/students), £4 (families)*
- *Shop*
- *Wheelchair access*

The Camden premises of this two-site museum (see separate entry below) tell the story of the history and religious life of Britain's Jewish community. The well appointed Ceremonial Art Gallery houses a fine collection of artifacts explaining and illustrating Jewish worship and festivals. Much of the silverware on display is of exceptionally high quality: delicate filigree amulets, elaborate 'spice towers', and a C16th Italian synagogue ark all stand testament to Jewish craftsmanship. The ground floor History Gallery includes a video presentation ('From the Cradle to the Grave'), which provides a useful introduction to ritual objects. A light-up map shows the ebb and flow of the Jewish community in Britain over the centuries, offering a graphic insight into the see-sawing between prosperity and persecution it has endured since the Norman Conquest.

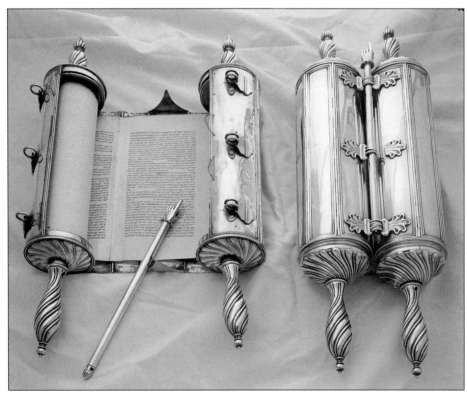

Torah Scrolls by Frederick Kandler, 1766, The Jewish Museum

The Jewish Museum

- 🏠 *80 East End Road, N3*
- ☎ *0181 349 1143*
- 🚌 *Transport: Finchley Central LU*
- 🕐 *Mon-Thurs 10.30-17.00; Sun 10.30-16.30 (closed Sundays in August and Jewish festivals)*
- ✈ *Admission £2, £1 concessions*
- ☕ *Café*
- ♿ *Wheelchair access (ground floor gallery only)*

This site of the Jewish museum focuses on the social history of Jewish people in London. Displays explore the Great Migration from Eastern Europe to the East End between 1881-1914 and the trades practised by the often poverty-stricken immigrants. Reconstructions of a furniture workshop and a tailor's workshop help set the scene along with evocative recorded reminiscences. A baker's trade union banner urging 'workers of the world unite' overlooks the proceedings.

Holocaust education forms a major part of the museum's work and the upper gallery is devoted to a permanent exhibition about the remarkable Leon Greenman – a British citizen who survived Auschwitz. Telling the story of an individual's experiences but placing them within the wider context of Nazi persecution, the exhibition is profoundly moving and comes highly recommended. Many of Mr Greenman's own photographs and personal possessions are included in the display – some of the most heart-wrenching items relating to his young son who, along with his Dutch wife, was killed within minutes of the family's arrival at Auschwitz. Now in his eighties and a veteran campaigner against racism and fascism, Mr Greenman is sometimes available to answer visitors' questions.

Keats House

- 🏠 *Keats Grove, NW3*
- ☎ *0171 435 2062*
- 🚌 *Transport: Belsize Park LU, Hampstead LU*
- 🕐 *April-Oct, Mon-Fri 10.00-13.00, 14.00-18.00, Sat 10.00-13.00, 14.00-17.00, Sun 14.00-17.00; Nov-March, Mon-Fri 13.00-17.00, Sat 10.00-13.00, 14.00-17.00, Sun 14.00-17.00*
- 🐚 *Admission free*
- ✈ *Shop*

Romantic poet par excellence, John Keats lived in this pretty Regency house from 1818-1820. Despite the onset of the TB which eventually killed him in 1821, Keats was at the height of his poetic powers during these years. It was here, sitting in the garden, that he penned his 'Ode to a Nightingale' and here too that he met and fell in love with Fanny Brawne. Memorabilia of their shortlived but intense relationship are displayed in the house – passionate letters, locks of hair and the garnet engagement ring Keats gave to her. Other exhibits explore different aspects of the poet's tragically short life and the manuscripts on display include a scrawled letter from William Wordsworth and an elegaic autograph poem by Thomas Hardy entitled 'At a house in Hampstead'. Furnished with authentic Regency pieces and surrounded by well-tended gardens, the house is understated but atmospheric. A 45 minute audio tour can be hired for a small charge.

nb. At the time of going to press Keats House is closed for major building repairs. No date for re-opening has been set.

MUSEUMS - NORTH

The London Canal Museum

⌨ *12-13 New Wharf Road, N1*

✆ *0171 713 0836*

🚌 *Transport: King's Cross St Pancras LU*

🕐 *Tues-Sun 1.00-16.40*

🏛 *Admission £2.50 (Adults),*
£1.25 (Concessions)

🛍 *Shop*

Overlooking the murky waters of Regent's Canal, the LCM celebrates the history of London's 'silent highway' from its heyday as a bustling trade route to its more recent role as a tourist trail. Visitors can experience at first hand the cramped conditions endured by canal folk in part of a restored narrowboat, admire the florid style of their decorative art and find out how canal locks work.

The building was once a Victorian ice house owned by ice cream entrepreneur Carlo Gatti and a massive, still only partially excavated ice pit dominates the far end of the ground floor. Displays covering London's ice trade and the history of ice cream explain its cavernous presence in this canalside warehouse, and upstairs in the former stables visitors can sit back and enjoy a video trip along the canal and help themselves to a DIY hot drink. The shop is small but well-stocked with relevant, reasonably-priced souvenirs, including books about boats and canals and a range of colourful hand-painted canalware.

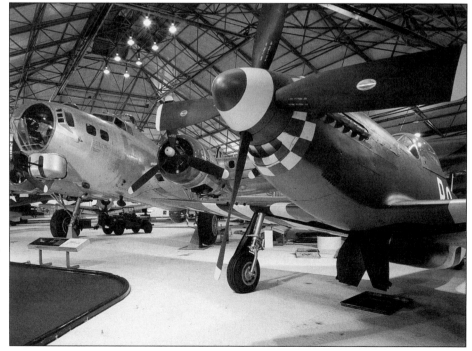

Royal Air Force Museum

Royal Air Force Museum

🖼 *Grahame Park Way, NW9*
☎ *0181 205 2266*
☎ *0181 205 9191 (24 hr information line)*
🚌 *Transport: Colindale LU*
🕐 *Daily 10.00-18.00*
💷 *Admission £5.85 (adults), £2.95*
   (unemployed, students, children),
   £4.40 (OAPs), £15 (families)
🛍 *Shop,*
☕ *Café and picnic areas*
♿ *Wheelchair access*

It's probably just as well that the admission charge to this, the National Museum of Aviation, includes a free return visit within 6 months – there's too much to see in a single day. Set on 10 acres of what was once Hendon aerodrome, the museum's two WWI hangars are now home to over 70 aircraft from skeletal bi-planes to streamlined jets. Telling the story of aviation from first principles to latest developments like the Eurofighter project, the emphasis is mainly military (although some civilian aircraft like the fun-sized, foldaway Hawker Cygnet do feature).

With planes stretching as far as the eye can see, the museum offers an impressive show case of the conservator's art – among the star exhibits is an immaculately restored Fokker D7 from 1917, resplendent in purple, green and black camouflage. Raised walkways let visitors look inside the cockpits of planes like the Phantom all-weather jet fighter or the inter-war Supermarine Southampton flying boat, while the 'touch and try' Provost lets eager aviationheads loose on the controls of a modern jet trainer. 'Top Trumps' veterans will relish the technical specifications which accompany each plane, and there's a Flight Simulator (£1.50 extra) for thrill-seekers.

Gargantuan aircraft like the Wellington and the Lancaster dominate the Bomber Command Hall, which scrutinizes the development of bombers and bombing.

Prize for the spookiest exhibit goes to the ghostly, water-stained wreck of a Halifax bomber, dredged up from the Norwegian fjord where it had lain since the 1940's. A reconstruction of a bombed-out industrial plant and photographs of the aftermath of the Dambuster raids are sobering reminders of the destructive capability of these giants of the air. Interspersed with the planes are training versions of missiles such as the sinister-sounding 'Yellow Sun' thermo-nuclear device.

A sequence of tableaux explain the background to the outbreak of war and Britain's 'finest hour' in the 'Battle of Britain Hall'. Many of the planes included in this section are German models like the Junkers 88, and there's even an Italian Fiat plane. A fragment of Rudolph Hess's wrecked Messerschmitt and Herman Goering's decorations and awards are among the more esoteric exhibits here. Tribute is paid to the 'Few' and the uniforms and medals of distinguished airmen are also displayed.

Amid all the hardware, the human element is never overlooked: throughout the museum are memorials and testaments to airmen and women from Great War to Gulf War. A quiet moment of contemplation can be snatched in the prefab RAF chapel from the Falkland Islands or besides the Spitfire flown by Flying Officer James Nicholson, winner of the only Fighter Command VC. Other displays highlight the roles played by test pilots, ground staff, the WAAF, and that major contribution to air safety – the ejector seat.

The Wings restaurant is on standby all day to cope with the inevitable hunger pangs but for those bringing packed lunches, there are pleasant picnics areas inside and out. The museum shop has more Airfix models than you can shake a stick at, and a wide range of aviation books and videos.

MUSEUMS - NORTH

MUSEUMS - NORTH

The Stephens Collection

⊡ *Avenue House, East End Road, N3*
◐ *0181 346 7812*
🚌 *Transport: Finchley Central LU*
🕐 *Tues-Thurs 14.00-16.30*
🏛 *Admission free*
🖵 *Refreshment kiosk*
♿ *Wheelchair access*

The history of writing materials and the story of the Stephens Ink Company are displayed on the ground floor of the house once owned by Henry 'Inky' Stephens.

2, Willow Road

⊡ *Willow Road, NW3*
◐ *0171 435 6166*
🚌 *Transport: Hampstead LU*
🕐 *3 Apr-1 Nov:*
   Thurs, Fri and Sat 12.00-17.00
☞ *Guided tours every 45 mins*
   (1 hour duration)
🏛 *Admission £3.60*

A Modern Movement interpretation of a terraced house, 2 Willow Road is as about as far from the stereotype of a National Trust property as it's possible to get. Set in leafy Hampstead, it was built by architect Erno Goldfinger in 1937 and remained his family's home until 1994. The stylish modernist aesthetic of the building is matched by its contents – along with furniture and toys designed by Goldfinger are works of art by Henry Moore, Bridget Riley, Max Ernst and Marcel Duchamp. Goldfinger's uncompromising approach is not everyone's cup of tea – his Trellick Tower in North Kensington remains controversial and it's no coincidence that Ian Fleming named one of 007's adversaries after the architect.

SOUTH

The Black Cultural Archives

- 🖃 *378 Coldharbour Lane, SW9*
- ✆ *0171 738 4591*
- 🚌 *Transport: Brixton LU*
- 🕔 *Mon-Sat 10.30-17.50 (museum)*
- 🦪 *Admission free*
- 🛍 *Shop*
- ♿ *Wheelchair access*

The museum hosts changing exhibitions and displays of work by black artists, while the archives (open by appointment, Mon-Fri 10.30-16.00) hold a range of material charting the history of black people in Britain.

Brunel Exhibition Rotherhithe

- 🖃 *Tunnel Road, SE16*
- 🚌 *Transport: Rotherhithe LU*
- 🕔 *First Sun every month and every Sun between Easter and end Sept 12.00-16.00*
- 🦪 *Admission £2 (adults), £1 (concessions), £5 (families)*
- 🛍 *Shop*
- ☕ *Refreshments*
- ♿ *Wheelchair access*

It took father and son team Marc and Isambard Brunel eighteen years to build the world's first under-river tunnel, linking Rotherhithe on the south side of the Thames to Wapping on the north. Located in the original Engine House, this museum commemorates their achievement (still used by London Underground's East London Line) and contains the only surviving example of a 'compound horizontal V steam' pumping engine built by J & G Rennie in 1885.

The Crystal Palace Museum

- 🖃 *Anerley Hill, Upper Norwood, SE19*
- ✆ *0181 676 0700*
- 🚌 *Transport: Crystal Palace Station*
- 🕔 *Sun and Bank Holidays 11.00-17.00*
- 🦪 *Admission free*
- 🛍 *Shop*

Hugely popular in its day, the Crystal Palace hosted everything from the Great Exhibition of 1851 to fun fairs and football cup finals before burning down in 1936. Dedicated to keeping its flame (as it were) alive, this museum is housed in the last surviving building constructed by the Crystal Palace Company. Numerous photos and artifacts tell the story of this glorified greenhouse and books and souvenirs relating to the palace are available from the museum's shop.

Cuming Museum

- 🖃 *155-157 Walworth Road, SE17*
- ✆ *0171 701 1342*
- 🚌 *Transport: Elephant and Castle LU*
- 🕔 *Tues-Sat 10.00-17.00*
- 🦪 *Admission free*

Nice things do come in small packages at this museum of Southwark's history. Hailed as a 'British Museum in miniature' when it opened in 1906, the Cuming's unglamourous premises are also home to the extraordinary collections of Richard and Henry Syer Cuming. Men of eclectic taste, their collection is nothing if not diverse: Japanese fans and Scandinavian deities jostle alongside Egyptian mummies, Roman plumbing and the work of 'Billy' and 'Charley', two Victorian mudlarks who did brisk business forging medieval antiquities.

The local history displays romp through several centuries of Southwark's past and have their fair share of curiosities. Bizarre, bygone superstitions to ensure health and wealth are the focus of the

MUSEUMS - SOUTH

Lovett Collection whilst among the C18th costumes there's a picturesque dentist's cap – trimmed with several mouthfuls of human teeth. A mechanical cow and a stuffed bear feature among the larger artifacts.

Primary school groups can get their hands on some of these treasures during special handling sessions – adult groups have to make do with tours on the Cumings and their collections. Plans are afoot to open a new museum of Southwark History, combining the interactivity of the Livesey Museum (see p.67) and the objects from the Cuming.

The Cutty Sark

- 🖼 *King William Walk, SE10*
- ☏ *0181 858 3445*
- 🚌 *Transport: Greenwich BR*
- ⏰ *Daily 10.00-18.00 (winter 10.00-17.00)*
- 💷 *Admission £3.50 (adults), £2.50 (concessions), £8.50 (families)*
- 📦 *Shop*

Even confirmed land-lubbers should be able to handle the Cutty Sark, moored as she is in dry dock by the Thames at Greenwich. With her sleek lines, soaring masts and elaborate rigging the last remaining tea clipper ship makes a stirring sight.

A concise display in the 'tween deck' tells the story of the Cutty Sark, the British mania for fresh China tea which she served, her record-breaking voyages, the rivalry between other clippers and the fateful impact of steam and the building of the Suez Canal on sail ships.

Down in the hold 'Nannie', the Cutty Sark's original figure head presides over a collection of merchant ship figure heads. Mostly of the 'buxom beauty' variety, their robust carving and vibrant colours are fetchingly vulgar. Up on the top deck the officers' woodpanelled saloon is the very picture of Victorian plushness but then even the crew's quarters look reasonably comfy – not a hammock in sight here.

Although with her gleaming brass fittings and neatly coiled ropes the Cutty Sark looks ship-shape, she is in fact about two years into a major restoration programme. Thanks to work already carried out, visitors can take home a piece of maritime history in the form of key rings made from part of the Cutty Sark's original metal foremast (£3.95). These and other nautically-inspired souvenirs are available from the cheesily-titled 'Bo'sun's Locker' shop. Guided tours are available but need to be pre-booked.

The Cutty Sark

The Fan Museum

🖃 *12 Crooms Hill, SE10*
🕾 *0181 858 7879/0181 305 1441*
🚌 *Transport: Greenwich BR*
🕙 *Tues-Sat 11.00-16.30; Sun 12 noon-16.30*
🦪 *Admission £3 (adults), £2 (concessions)*
(Tues14.00-16.30 free entry for
OAPs and disabled)
🕸 *Shop*
♿ *Wheelchair access*

Set in two immaculately restored Georgian houses, this small museum oozes gentility from every pore – from its tasteful décor and charming volunteer staff to its award-winning lavatories (the nicest I've ever seen in a museum).

As well as fans, painted fan leaves feature in the permanent display – a rare C17th example depicts a somewhat glum bunch of French royals at a birthday party – but the history and craft of fan-making are also explored. The fans themselves range from an exquisitely carved ivory Chinese fan, to Eskimo 'finger fans' and modern electric numbers. Clocking in at over 40 minutes, the audio tour is over long but gives a useful introduction to the collection, even if you don't listen to the whole thing. Changing themed exhibitions are held in the upstairs gallery – past shows have included fans from around the world and children's fans – and the museum also runs fan-making workshops.

Fans appear in a variety of guises in the imaginatively stocked museum shop. Fan fayre on offer includes pricey jewellery, natty folding fan hats (£9.95), greetings cards and toiletries, with very simple fans starting at £1.50 and going up to elegant contemporary French designs at £35. Frustratingly, the conservatory at the back doesn't contain a café but, this being Greenwich, there's no shortage of good eating opportunities within easy walking distance.

MUSEUMS - SOUTH

Fan Museum

MUSEUMS - SOUTH

Greenwich Borough Museum

- 222 Plumstead High Street, SE18
- 0181 855 3240
- Transport: Plumstead BR
- Mon 14.00-19.00, Tues, Thurs, Fri, Sat
  10.00-13.00, 14.00-17.00
- Admission free
- Small sales point

A community museum illustrating the history of the borough and surrounding areas. Permanent displays illustrate local life – human and otherwise – from prehistory to the present day and include archaeological finds and natural history specimens as well as an extensive collection of household objects. The museum's long-established Education Service runs a Saturday Club for children aged 5 yrs and upwards and during school holidays, workshops for both adults and children.

Horniman Museum

The Horniman Museum & Gardens

- 100 London Road, Forest Hill SE23
- 0181 699 1872
- Transport: Forest Hill BR
- Mon-Sat 10.30-17.30,
  Sun 14.00-17.30 (museum),
- Daily 8.00-dusk (gardens)
- Admission free
- Shop
- Café
- Wheelchair access (contact in advance)

Although firmly rooted in its South London community, the Horniman is much more than a purely 'local' museum. With displays embracing natural history, ethnography and a vast collection of musical instruments, this popular museum revels in its diversity – and its enthusiasm is catching.

Billed as the 'aquarium of the future', 'Living Waters' showcases a variety of endangered watery habitats, with the emphasis on conservation. Visitors can follow the journey of a river upstream from mouth to source, peer into the dark waters of a flooded forest pool or wonder at the brilliance and fragility of a coral reef. In these aquatic stage sets the fish – flamboyantly costumed clown fish and stately seahorses – are consummate performers and usually have a captive audience. The crustacea-filled rockpool even has high tide and low tide.

A veritable menagerie of stuffed animals populate the Natural History section, centred around an enormous, somewhat elderly walrus. Displays explore topics such as evolution as well as Forest Hill's own flora and fauna, making the Horniman a well-structured, free alternative to the Natural History Museum.

Masks and puppets from around the world are a highlight of the ethnographic collection. Glove puppets and Sicilian marionettes vie for attention alongside a cast of shadow puppets from Turkey, whose characters rejoice in politically incorrect names like 'The Boastful Dwarf Odd Job Man' and 'The Quarrelsome Woman of Easy Virtue'. In the Music Room visitors can admire thousands of musical instruments from across the globe and through the ages, from the sleek Stratocaster electric guitar to authentic Hawaiian instruments such as the 'nutshell whistle'. Interactive computers play the sounds that the various instruments make and provide more detailed information about their history and how they are made. Toys, animals and instruments are all up for grabs in the museum's regular 'Hands on our...' workshops – a good way of getting round the problem of case-bound exhibits.

Ironically, what sounds the most innovative part of the museum – the Centre for Understanding the Environment (CUE) – is slightly disappointing. Despite sporting impeccably green credentials (with a grass roof and an interior like a Scandinavian log cabin) the exhibits here were a bit thin on the ground – perhaps I went on the wrong day. The no-frills café means you won't starve but the Horniman's 16 acres of gardens offer an ideal venue for a picnic and there's even the Railway Nature Trail for green-fingered folk.

The Livesey Museum

- 🖼 *682 Old Kent Road, SE15*
- 🕐 *0171 639 5604*
- 🚌 *Transport: Elephant and Castle (then bus)*
- 🕐 *Tues-Sat 10.00-17.00*
- 🦋 *Admission free*
- 🛍 *Shop and Picnic area*
- ♿ *Limited wheelchair access*

A children's museum for under 12's with a changing programme of temporary exhibitions. A recent exhibition 'Going Underground' offered kids the chance to find out about tunnels – from earthworms' lairs to the Jubilee Line extension.

Metropolitan Police Traffic Museum

- 🖼 *34 Aitken Road, Catford, SE6*
- 🕐 *0181 284 5909*
- 🚌 *Transport: Bellingham BR*
- 🕐 *Open by appointment only*
- 🦋 *Admission free*
- ♿ *Wheelchair Access*

Housed in an operational police headquarters, this museum covers the history of the Metropolitan Police traffic patrols. Its displays include old police vehicles, uniforms, photos and paraphernalia. Visits are subject to cancellation for operational reasons.

The Museum of Artillery in the Rotunda

- 🖼 *Repository Road, SE18*
- 🕐 *0181 316 5402 (Curator)*
- 🚌 *Transport: Woolwich Arsenal BR*
- 🕐 *Mon-Fri 12.30-16.00 (ring to confirm)*
- 🦋 *Admission free*
- ♿ *Wheelchair access*

The Rotunda started life as a huge replica bell tent, used as a party venue by the fun loving Prince Regent before being moved to Woolwich and converted into a permanent building. It now makes an elegant home for a diverse collection of artillery which embraces early gun-making experiments to more recent hardware like the LANCE missile system. Some of the more esoteric exhibits include part of the Iraqi 'supergun' and a 'dragon gun' from the palace of the King of Burma.

A museum of artillery with more fully interpreted displays is being developed at the Royal Arsenal at Woolwich and is set to open in 2001. The Rotunda collections will form a large part of the new museum, which will also contain much of the Royal Artillery Regimental museum (now closed).

MUSEUMS - SOUTH

National Maritime Museum

- ⌗ *Greenwich, SE10*
- ☎ *0181 858 4422*
- ☎ *0181 312 6565 (recorded information)*
- 🚌 *Transport: Maze Hill BR*
- 🕐 *Mon-Sun 10.00-17.00*
- 💰 *Admission £5.00 (adults), £2.50 (children) (includes entry to Queen's House and Old Royal Observatory)*
- 🛍 *Shop*
- ☕ *Café*
- ♿ *Wheelchair access (ring first for details)*

A testament to when Britannia really did rule the waves, the NMM covers every aspect of ships and seafaring, from prehistoric times to the present day. At the time of writing, the museum is in the throes of a massive development programme and many of its galleries have been closed for building work. The scheme will create 11 new galleries, allowing more of the museum's extensive nautical collection to be shown whilst ensuring better facilities and easier access for visitors.

It is hoped that the 'C20th Seapower', 'Nelson', and 'All Hands' galleries will remain open until the project is completed in Spring 1999 and that they are still worth a visit in conjunction with the other museums under the NMM's auspices. 'Seapower' is awash with power-ful images of the ocean: paintings of top sea dogs juxtaposed with films of topics such as the changing role of sea trade and the Battle of Jutland. For those who want to play battleships there's an excellent reconstruction of a frigate's operation room, equipped with surface ship command simulators. The Nelson Gallery provides a detailed exploration of one of Britain's greatest naval heros. The coat Nelson wore at Trafalgar is on display – complete with bullet hole and bloody breeches – and if that doesn't stir the imagination a computer-animated

Captain Horatio Nelson, National Maritime Museum

reconstruction of the battle should do the trick. 'All Hands' is aimed squarely at sea-puppies and, with some genuinely hands on exhibits, is great fun. Aspiring admirals can signal to each other using flags, morse code or two-way radio, learn what it's like to work deep underwater in total darkness or discover what Vikings ate on their 'cruises'. 'The Bosun's Kitchen' provides more appetising fare (with décor straight out of a cross channel ferry), and the shop stocks such delights as ships in bottles and stationery made from recycled sea charts.

Old Royal Observatory

- 🖃 *Greenwich, SE10*
- 🕾 *0181 858 4422*
- 🕾 *0181 312 6565 (recorded information)*
- 🚌 *Transport: Greenwich BR, Maze Hill BR*
- 🕐 *Mon-Sun 10.00-17.00*
- 🥾 *Admission £5.00 (adults),*
  £2.50 (children)
  (includes entry to the Queen's House and
  National Maritime Museum)
- 🛍 *Shop*
- ♿ *Wheelchair access (ring first for details)*

A short sharp walk up the hill from the Queen's House and Maritime Museum brings you to a cluster of buildings which look more like a stable block than an observatory (although the big white 'onion' dome is a bit of a give away).

Straddling the meridian line (at 0 degrees longitude) and home to Greenwich Mean Time, the Observatory can claim to be 'the centre of time and space'. Visitors line up to photograph each other with one foot in the East, the other in the West. The 'Camera Obscura' is much more entertaining: a revolving panorama of Greenwich projected live onto a table in the middle of the room. Next door, Flamsteed House contains the spartan apartments of the Astronomers Royal and the Octagon Room, a rare survival of an interior by Sir Christopher Wren. Instruments for measuring time and space are also on display and include the watch which cracked the navigators' problem of finding longitude. If you get to the Observatory before 1pm, look out for the Time Ball which drops at that exact time each day to let ships on the Thames set their chronometers.

Old Royal Observatory

MUSEUMS - SOUTH

The Tulip Staircase, The Queens House

The Pumphouse Educational Museum/Rotherhithe Heritage Museum

⌖ Lavender Road, SE16
☎ 0171 231 2976
🚌 Transport: Buses: P11 Waterloo to Peckham; 225 Lewisham to Brunel Road; Rotherhithe, Surrey Quays LU
🕐 Mon-Fri 10.30-15.00
⚜ Public entrance by donation
✧ Shop
🖵 Lunch area
♿ Wheelchair access

Artifacts found along the Thames' foreshore recount the story of one of London's oldest villages at this local history museum. The result of 10 years of beachcombing by local man Ron Goode, the collection includes dockers' tools, coins and everyday objects dating from pre-Roman times. Housed in the Lavender Pond Pumphouse, the museum is surrounded by a nature park complete with trails, assorted wildlife and a pond.

The Puppet Centre

⌖ BAC, Lavender Hill, SW11
☎ 0171 228 5335
🚌 Transport: Clapham Junction BR
🕐 Mon-Fri 14.00-18.00, some Sat afternoons by appointment
⚜ Admission Free
✧ Shop
🖵 Café
♿ Wheelchair access

Changing displays from the centre's collection of puppets, and a reference library on puppetry and related art forms.

70

The Queen's House

- 🖼 *Greenwich, SE10*
- ☎ *0181 858 4422*
- ☎ *0181 293 9618 (recorded information)*
- 🚌 *Transport: Maze Hill BR*
- 🕓 *Mon-Sat 10.00-17.00, Sun 12.00-17.00*
- 🍽 *Admission £5.00 (adults), £2.50 (children) (includes entry to Old Royal Observatory and Maritime Museum)*

Built for Charles I's wife, Queen Henrietta Maria, this gracious residence holds the double distinction of being the first classical building in England and the first to boast a flight of cantilevered stairs. It has been sumptuously restored, with the his'n'hers throne rooms being only slightly overshadowed by the Queen's Bedchamber with its whacky silver and purple décor. What's nice about this stately home though is its tranquil, Italianate atmosphere and 'backstage' rooms: the odd little antechambers and closets that evoke the daily existence of its inhabitants more clearly than its works of art and ritzy brocaded wallpaper.

Anne Cecil, Rangers House

Ranger's House

- 🖼 *Chesterfield Walk, SE10*
- ☎ *0181 853 0035*
- 🚌 *Transport: Greenwich BR, Blackheath BR*
- 🕓 *Daily 1 April – 31 Oct 10.00-18.00; 1 Nov-31 March Wed-Sun 10.00-16.00. Closed 13.00-14.00 (depending on staff availability).*
- 🍽 *Admission £2.50 (adults), £1.90 (concessions), £1.30 (under 16's), English Heritage members free*
- 🛍 *Shop*
- ♿ *Wheelchair access to ground floor*

Although the Dolmetsch collection of musical instruments is no longer here, Ranger's House is still home to the impressive Suffolk Collection of portraits. Works include Sergeant's glamourous canvas of Margaret Hyde and Van Dyck's tender portrait of Charles I's children, but the real highlights are the Jacobean portraits which line the vast expanse of the Saloon. The paintings' rich colours, crisp handling and the gorgeous costumes of their aristocratic sitters contrast with the rather run down air of the house. Visitors en route to or from the nearby Fan Museum (p.65) should look out for the portraits of twins Diana and Anne Cecil, with their matching outfits and fans at the ready. Outside in the Coach House, the Architectural Study Centre displays fragments salvaged from demolished London houses: everything from coal hole covers to classical columns to a patented papier-mâché ceiling rose.

MUSEUMS - SOUTH

Wandsworth Museum

- 🖳 *The Courthouse, 11 Garratt Lane, SW18*
- 🕐 *0181 871 7074*
- 🚌 *Transport: East Putney LU*
- 🕐 *Tues-Sat 10.00-17.00, Sun 14.00-17.00*
- 🍴 *Admission free*
- 🛍 *Shop*
- ♿ *Wheelchair access*

The former Surrey County Courthouse is now home to the new Wandsworth Museum of local history. A visually striking exhibition tells the 'Story of Wandsworth' and offers visitors the chance to become a Celtic chieftain, rub a medieval brass or go 'through the keyhole' of a terraced house in Battersea to see what its yuppy residents have done to it. In the courtroom, 'The Villages of Wandsworth' takes a more detailed look at the old village centres of the borough, while a variety of temporary displays supplement the two permanent exhibitions. The museum shop stocks a range of local history publications and souvenirs. Winner of an Access award for its facilities, the museum has full wheelchair access.

The Wimbledon Lawn Tennis Museum

- 🖳 *Church Road, SW19*
- 🕐 *0181 946 6131*
- 🚌 *Transport: Wimbledon LU/BR*
- 🕐 *Tues-Sat 10.30-17.00, Sun 14.00-17.00*
  (during the Championships open only to those visiting the tournament)
- 🍴 *Admission £2.50 (adults), £1.50 (OAP'S, students, under 16s)*
- ☕ *Café*
- 🛍 *Shop*
- ♿ *Wheelchair access*

It's hard to believe it now, but lawn tennis was once just a glorified garden party game, rejoicing in the preposterous brand name of 'Sphairistiké'. This museum, based at the famous All England Lawn Tennis Club, follows the development of the game from genteel pastime to mega-bucks international industry (and all this thanks to the invention of the lawn mower and the bouncy rubber ball). Tableaux recreate the early days of tennis – right down to the tea-time cucumber sandwiches – while comprehensive displays of tennis equipment show how the game evolved into today's hi-speed, hi-tech sport. On-court fashions range from full length Edwardian dresses to Billy Jean King's sequined micro-minis and there are profiles, television footage and memorabilia of past and present tennis stars. Wimbledon's glittering prizes – the Ladies' Singles salver and Mens' Singles cup – are among the exhibits and for those who missed out, the video room plays highlights of last year's Championships. The museum shop stocks souvenirs and Wimbledon leisurewear but if purple and green aren't your thing, the well-appointed tea room serves light lunches and traditional cream teas.

The Wimbledon Society Museum

- 🖳 *22 Ridgway, SW19*
- 🕐 *0181 296 9914*
- 🚌 *Transport: Wimbledon LU*
- 🕐 *Sat 14.30-17.00 (at other times by appointment)*
- 🍴 *Admission free*
- 🛍 *Shop*

The three thousand year history of Wimbledon in pictures, words and objects. The museum's large archive contains over 2,500 photographs and many paintings, prints, maps and manuscripts.

Wimbledon Windmill Museum

- 🖳 *Windmill Road,*
  Wimbledon Common, SW19
- 🕿 *0181 947 2825*
- 🚌 *Transport: Wimbledon LU, Putney LU*
- 🕐 *Sat, Sun and Public Holidays April-Oct*
  14.00-17.00
- 🍽 *£1 (adults), 50p (children/Concessions)*
- ☕ *Café*

What better place to tell the story of windmills and windmilling than in a windmill itself? Models as well as original machinery bring the narrative to life and teacher's notes on the history, science and technology of windmills are available. If it's all too much of a grind, the café's just next door.

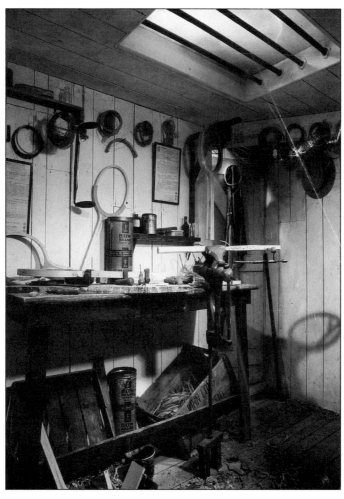

Racket Makers Workshop, c1900, Wimbledon Lawn Tennis Museum

WEST

The Alexander Fleming Laboratory Museum

⌨ *St Mary's Hospital, Praed St, W2*
☏ *0171 725 6528*
🚌 *Transport: Paddington LU*
🕐 *Mon-Thurs 10.00-13.00,*
☞ *Guided tours on the hour; open by appointment only Mon-Thurs 2.00-17.00, Fri 10.00-17.00*
🍽 *Admission £2 (adults), £1 (concessions)*
◈ *Shop*

It was in this tiny, old-fashioned laboratory that Alexander Fleming discovered penicillin – a storm in a petri dish that transformed its discoverer into a national hero and earned him a Nobel Prize.

A very distant relation to today's pristine white boxes, the laboratory is an accurate reconstruction of Fleming's workplace (although the original culture plate is housed at the British Library). Volunteers guides, some of them retired medical staff who knew Fleming personally, talk visitors through the momentous – and completely accidental – discovery of penicillin. A concise, well-presented exhibition charts the development of penicillin from mystery mould to life-saving wonder drug and the impact of antibiotics on modern medicine. The displays also recount the details of Fleming's life and career – including reproductions of the bizarre 'germ' paintings he created.

Carlyle's House

⌨ *24 Cheyne Row, SW3*
☏ *0171 352 7087*
🚌 *Transport: Sloane Square LU*
🕐 *29 Mar-2 Nov: Wed-Sun and Bank Holiday Mon 11.00-17.00*
🍽 *Admission £3 (adults), £1.50 (children)*

This desirable Chelsea building was home to Victorian historian Thomas Carlyle. Although Carlyle's star has waned in this century, he was a hugely influential writer in his day, called on by the likes of Tennyson, Dickens, George Eliot and Chopin (who played Mrs Carlyle's piano). Today's visitors can follow in their footsteps, soaking up the atmosphere of these intimate rooms which still contain their original furnishings, together with Carlyle's books and personal effects.

The Chelsea Physic Garden

⌨ *66 Royal Hospital Road, SW3*
☏ *0171 352 5646*
🚌 *Sloane Square LU*
🕐 *5 April-25 Oct Wed 12.00-17.00, Sun 14.00-18.00; closed winter*
🍽 *Admission £3.50 (adults), £1.80 (concessions)*
◈ *Shop*
♿ *Wheelchair access*

Despite the roar of traffic from the neighbouring Chelsea Embankment, this formal historic walled garden is a magical place. Founded in 1673 as a botanic garden to promote the study of medicinal plants, the Physic Garden continues the same role today and is filled with therapeutic flora from around the world. Most specimens, from traditional medicinal plants like verbena to major medicinal plants such as evening primrose, are clearly labelled with their botanical classification and place of natural origin, as well as what ailments they treat. Enjoying a balmy micro-climate, the 3½ acre garden also cultivates rare and tender plants and boasts one of the earliest rock gardens in England. A profusion of benches line the scrunchy gravel paths and on a sunny summer's day there are few nicer places to be in London.

MUSEUMS - WEST

Chiswick House

- ⌨ *Burlington Lane, W4*
- ☏ *0181 995 0508*
- 🚌 *Transport: Turnham Green LU*
- 🕐 *22 March-31 Oct, daily 10.00-18.00.*
  1 Nov-31 March Wed-Sun 10.00-16.00
- 🦪 *Admission £2.50 (adults), £1.90*
  (concessions), £1.30 (children)
- 🛍 *Shop*

The last word in classical chic when it was built in the 1720's, Chiswick House is still a sumptuously stylish pad by any standards. Owner-architect Lord Burlington was inspired by the architecture of Ancient Rome and the austere symmetry of his villa is typical of his rigorous approach to design. The decadent-sounding Blue Velvet Room is one of several fine interiors for which manicured Italianate gardens are the perfect natural foil. An audio tour, introductory film and exhibition are included in the admission charge.

The Commonwealth Experience

- ⌨ *Kensington High Street, W8*
- ☏ *0171 603 4535*
- 🚌 *Transport: Kensington High Street LU*
- 🕐 *Daily 10.00-17.00*
- 🦪 *Admission £4.45 (adults),*
  £2.95 (children), £11.95 (families)
- 🛍 *Shop*
- ☕ *Café*
- ♿ *Wheelchair access*

Recently revamped, the visitor attraction formerly known as the Commonwealth Institute now boasts crowd-pleasers such as a simulated helicopter flight over Malaysia. Sadly, on the day of my visit the heliride was out of order but I did enjoy the 'Asian A-Z' pre-flight briefing which took in all things Oriental from Abacus to Zero.

Less well integrated was 'Interactive World', a hotch-potch of hands on exhibits for kids. Bearing a remarkable similarity to

Chiswick House

the Science Museum's Launch Pad (see p.85), these supposedly recreate natural phenomena from across the Commonwealth but seemed to exist more for the sake of their 'interactivity'.

The bulk of the 'experience' consists of displays from each of the 50 countries which make up the Commonwealth. With a tendency to lapse into bland tourist board style, peppered with statements like "[insert name of country] has much to offer the visitor", the displays are a mildly pleasant, if undemanding variant on armchair travel. Those of a more active disposition can climb aboard a cowboy saddle (Canada), operate a life-saving borehole pump (Africa) or try to decipher some of the Caribbean's many dialects. Two gallery spaces continue the Institute's tradition of exhibiting work by Commonwealth artists and Commonwealth information, and news is available at the Library and Resource Centre. Both the café and shop are undistinguished, given the Commonwealth cuisine and produce that could have been showcased here.

MUSEUMS - *WEST*

75

Gunnersbury Park Museum

⬚ *Gunnersbury Park, Popes Lane, W3*
☎ *0181 992 1612*
🚌 *Transport: Acton Town LU*
🕐 *Daily, April-Oct 13.00-17.00 (weekends and bank holidays 13.00-18.00); Nov-March 13.00-16.00 (weekends and bank holidays 13.00-17.00)*
🍽 *Admission free*
☕ *Café*
♿ *Wheelchair access*

Local history museums don't come much grander than this. Once the home of the Rothschild family, the richly decorated rooms of Gunnersbury Mansion are now furnished with exhibitions about Ealing's and Hounslow's past. Period clothing is displayed in the costume gallery, while the Rothschild's regal carriages help to illustrate transport in days gone by. A copious collection of domestic objects and the fully restored Victorian kitchens give a 'below stairs' insight into how a large household was run. A lively and varied programme of changing exhibitions highlights particular aspects of local history – everything from market gardening to travellers in Ealing.

Hogarth's House

⬚ *Hogarth Lane, Great West Road, W4*
☎ *0181 994 6757*
🚌 *Transport: Turnham Green LU*
🕐 *Tues-Fri 13.00-17.00 (Nov-Mar 13.00-16.00), Sat and Sun 13.00-18.00 (Nov-Mar 13.00-17.00)*
🍽 *Admission free*
🛍 *Shop*
♿ *Wheelchair access (ground floor only)*

Once the country home of painter William Hogarth, this early C18th house has been fully restored and redisplayed for the centenary of the artist's birth in 1697. Often regarded as the founder of British painting, Hogarth's fame now rests on the detailed social observation and scathing moral commentaries of engravings such as 'The Rake's Progress' and 'The Harlot's Progress'. These and many other of Hogarth's prints are displayed as part of an exhibition telling the story of his life and work.

Kensington Palace State Apartments

⬚ *Kensington, W8*
☎ *0171 937 9561*
🚌 *Transport: Queensway LU, Notting Hill LU, High Street Kensington LU, Gloucester Road LU*
🕐 *From 1 May 1998, daily 10.00-18.00*
🍽 *Admission £7.50 (adults), £5.90 (concessions), £5.30 (Children)*
☞ *Guided tours throughout day, starting at 10.15*
🛍 *Shop*
☕ *Café*

Kensington Palace was snapped up by royal house hunters and joint monarchs William and Mary in 1689 when it was still humble Nottingham House. Remodelled by Sir Christoper Wren, this tidy red brick building (latterly the home of Diana, Princess of Wales) boasts illusory ceilings and staircase painted by William Kent, and a clutch of Old Master paintings in the recently restored King's Apartments. A permanent redisplay of the the vast Royal Ceremonial Dress Collection, which includes pieces such as George IV's coronation robes and the waistcoat worn by George III during his illness, opens in May 1998.

Leighton House Art Gallery & Museum

🖃 *12 Holland Park Road, W14*
📞 *0171 602 3316*
🚌 *Transport: High Street Kensington LU*
🕐 *Mon-Sat 11.00-17.30*
🐌 *Admission free*

This evocative haute-bohemian pad was once home to Frederic, Lord Leighton, the great classical painter of the Victorian age. Hung with paintings by the man himself and his Pre-Raphaelite pals Millais and Burne-Jones, and with ceramics by William de Morgan the house was designed as a palace devoted to art, and its darkly opulent interiors are spellbinding. Leighton's vast studio dominates the upper floor but the domed Arab Hall is the centrepiece of the house: a Moorish fantasia complete with gilt mosaic frieze, antique decorative tiles, lattice work window frames and gently-playing fountain. Guided tours take place every Wednesday and Thursday at noon – alternatively, an audio tour of the house costs £1.50, the illustrated guidebook £3.

Linley Sambourne House

🖃 *18 Stafford Terrace, W8*
📞 *0181 742 3438*
🚌 *Transport: High Street Kensington LU*
🕐 *March-Oct: Wed 10.00-16.00,*
   Sat 14.00-17.00
🐌 *Admission £3 (adults), £2.50 (OAP's)*

Jam packed with pictures, ornaments and knick-knacks of all sorts, this terraced house was the home of Punch illustrator and cartoonist Linley Sambourne. The artist's own photographs – the basis for many of his cartoons – can also be viewed in the bathroom.

The Arab Hall, Leighton House Museum

The London Toy and Model Museum

🖃 *21/23 Craven Hill, W2*
📞 *0171 706 8000*
📞 *0171 402 5222 (recorded information)*
🚌 *Transport: Paddington LU, Lancaster Gate LU, Queensway LU, Bayswater LU*
🕐 *Mon-Sat 10.00-17.30, Sun 11.00-17.30 (last admission 16.30)*
🐌 *Admission £4.95 (adults), £2.95 (4-16 yr olds), £13.50 (families), wheelchair users and under 4's free*
🛍 *Shop*
☕ *Café*
♿ *Wheelchair access (ground and basement only)*

With the emphasis just as much on models as on toys, this is a museum with adult appeal. Both works of art and labours of love, the models range from elaborate dioramas – like the room-sized working coal mine – to scale models of individual

MUSEUMS - *WEST*

steam engines. Transport is a predominate theme throughout and trains, cars, boats and aeroplanes are each given their own galleries. The distinction between toys and models is a nebulous one though and much of the information about exhibits – giving details of manufacturers etc. – is likely to interest adult enthusiasts rather than children.

But toys will be toys and there's lots of them here, both ancient and modern. There's a room devoted to dolls, including a rather stern 'Quaker lady' and the stupendously ugly 'Kaiser' baby of 1909. The oldest toy in the collection – a clay Roman gladiator doll – could be Action Man's distant cousin (although without the gripping hands and eagle eyes). Cuddlier playthings are well represented and as well as celebrating animal toys in general, the Forest Gallery features a teddy bears' picnic. As befits someone named after the nearby railway station, Paddington quite rightly gets a display case to himself (along with his spin-off merchandise).

The staple of many a rainy childhood afternoon, boardgames are not neglected either and visitors can pit their wits, strength or credulity against an assortment of old-fashioned slot machines in the popular 'Penny Arcade'. In time-honoured tradition, batteries are not included but a change machine is on hand to change new coins into old pennies (10p=1d).

Based in two converted Victorian townhouses, the museum's 20 themed galleries and numerous staircases (the lift only serves ground floor and basement) can get congested. However, the galleries are imaginatively designed (each one a life-sized reconstruction based on toys and models in the collection), and weather permitting, there's a carousel and train ride in the walled garden. The café serves basic, reasonably priced grub and the shop, parents will be relieved to know, also sells inexpensive items with an emphasis on traditional games and pastimes. A nappy-changing room is also available for when the excitement gets too much.

London Toy and Model Museum

Lord's Cricket Ground

⌕ *St John's Road, NW8*
☎ *0171 432 1033/0171 289 1611*
🚌 *Transport: St John's Wood LU*
🕐 *On match days museum open to match spectators only*
☞ *Tours of the ground (incl. museum) usually twice daily throughout year (except match days), please telephone for times.*
🍴 *Admission £5.80 (adults), £4.20 (concessions), £18 (families)*
☕ *Shop and tavern*
♿ *Partial wheelchair access*

Based at Lords, the home of cricket, Marylebone Cricket Club's museum is a haven for those who love the sound of leather against willow. For those less familiar with the game, displays chart over 400 years of cricketing history while full size model players demonstrate batting, bowling and wicket-keeping techniques. Unwieldy curved edge bats and two-stump wickets (which often let the ball straight through) date from the days when sheep kept the pitch in trim – more up to date clobber includes the pads, blazers, boots and caps of Sir Donald Bradman and Sir Jack Hobbs. Special exhibitions are mounted to mark particular anniversaries and honour visiting teams. A stuffed sparrow commemorates one of the game's smaller casualties (clean bowled in 1936) but pride of place undoubtedly goes to the Ashes – a permanent fixture in the museum regardless of whether Australia or England win. The first player to score 100 centuries, W.G. Grace is immortalised in paint, along with Wisden (he of the Almanack), Sir Garfield Sobers and Sir Colin Cowdrey. More paintings and memorabilia are displayed in the Long Room, the MCC's inner sanctum. Normally a male-only zone, this atmospheric club room can be viewed by visitors of both sexes on the tour only.

Cricket gear is stocked at the Lord's shop, along with a comprehensive selection of cricketing books and souvenirs ranging from floppy hats to pencil sharpeners. A small section marked 'Ladies Gifts' includes headscarves and hipflasks – must-haves, presumably, for the cricketing woman. Refreshments are available at the Lord's Tavern, the up-market on-site pub.

The Museum of Fulham Palace

⌕ *Bishops Avenue, SW6*
☎ *0171 736 3233*
🚌 *Transport: Putney Bridge LU*
🕐 *March-Oct, Wed-Sun 14.00-17.00; Nov-Feb Thurs-Sun 13.00-16.00; grounds open daily*
🍴 *Admission 50p (adults), 25p (concessions)*
🛍 *Shop*
♿ *Disabled access*

This small museum tells the sometimes bloody story, of the Bishops of London, their historic palace and its gardens. The ghost of Bishop Bonner is said to haunt the Tudor Courtyard but more tangible exhibits take the form of archaeological remains, gardening tools and Bishop Winnington-Ingram's bejewelled and embroidered mitre and cope. Benjamin West's pious portraits of Thomas a Becket and Margaret of Anjou are among the paintings on display.

The National Army Museum

⌕ *Royal Hospital Road, SW3*
☎ *0171 730 0717*
🚌 *Transport: Sloane Square LU*
🕐 *Mon-Sun 10.00-17.30*
🍴 *Admission free*
🛍 *Shop*
☕ *Café*
♿ *Wheelchair access*

A museum to gladden the heart of any 'Soldier, Soldier' fan. Unlike the Imperial War Museum (see p.23-24), whose subject is C20th conflict, the NAM focuses on the life of ordinary British and Commonwealth

MUSEUMS - WEST

soldiers and is appropriately situated next to the Royal Hospital, home of the Chelsea pensioners.

Starting with the crack-shot archers at Agincourt, the permanent displays chart the development of the modern soldier right up to the Cold War and beyond (including for example, artifacts from the war in Bosnia). 'The Nation in Arms' ably covers the period 1914-45, but for my money the best gallery follows the less well-trodden 'Road to Waterloo'. Filled with the weaponry and uniforms you might expect from a military museum, the gallery also features curiosities like a 50 metre square model of the Battle of Waterloo with a cast of 75,000 tin soldiers, and the skeleton of Napoleon's favourite charger at that same fateful

encounter. As elsewhere in the museum, startlingly realistic full-sized models of historic soldiers, from the doughty camp follower carrying her sick husband, to the umbrella-toting Dragoon, bring the stories to life.

Other displays explore the rise of the redcoat and the history of women in the army, while separate galleries show off the museum's impressive collections of uniforms and paintings – from portraits of soldiers such as the pub-loving Marquis of Granby, to action-packed battle scenes. A good selection of military books and knick-knacks can be found in the shop and although basic, the café is strategically placed to let you regroup your forces before doing battle with the well-heeled hordes of Chelsea.

Mortuary Sword, c1645-50, National Army Museum

The Natural History Museum

- 🖃 *Cromwell Road, SW7*
- 🕿 *0171 938 9123*
- 🚌 *Transport: South Kensington LU*
- 🕐 *Mon-Sat 10.00-17.50; Sun 11.00-17.50*
- 🍽 *Admission £6.00 (adults), £3.00 (children), £3.20 (concessions); (free entry after 16.30 Mon-Fri and after 17.00 weekends and bank holidays)*
- 🛍 *Shops*
- 🖵 *Cafés*
- ♿ *Wheelchair access*

One of South Kensington's 'Big Three', the Natural History Museum has been a London landmark for over a century. Famed for its dinosaur collection, the museum was, until recent years, in danger of becoming a fossil itself. Now with revamped displays in the Life Galleries and the 1996 opening of the new Earth Galleries, the Museum welcomes over 1.5 million visitors a year (despite the controversial introduction of admission charges) and supports a 300-strong team of research scientists behind the scenes.

Purpose built by Alfred Waterhouse, the museum building is worth a visit in its own right. While its elegant Romanesque arches conceal an iron and steel framework (the last word in Victorian innovation), the exterior sculptures of plants and animals form a Gothic curtain raiser to the exhibits inside – some of which are detailed below.

Dominated by the famous diplodocus skeleton, the Cromwell Road entrance hall introduces the 'wonders' of the museum. Eight exhibition bays house an item drawn from the museum's vast collection of over 68 million specimens, each accompanied by a multilingual touch screen computer which tells you where to find related exhibits, as well as acting as a more general guide.

Diplodocus has been shrewdly placed: I suspect many make 'Dinosaurs' their first port of call. It can't take many dinosaurs to fill a room, but this display is chock full of overgrown skeletons who all look ready to sample some human prey. A raised walkway brings you eyeball to eyeball with 'fearful lizards' like Dromaeosaurus, Triceratops and the mighty Tyrannosaurus Rex. Vicious claws, teeth, horns and spines abound in this gallery and you can see some of them in action in a life-size animated diorama of three Deinonychus ('terrible hand') tucking into a recently-deceased herbivore. On ground level, interactive displays and smaller exhibits ask 'What is a Dinosaur?' and look at possible reasons for their demise.

There's more animal magic, albeit of the stuffed variety in 'Mammals'. Flying mammals and mammals with pouches put in an appearance alongside more familiar species. The life-size model of a blue whale, slung from the ceiling, makes even the giraffe and elephant look like small fry. Films and hands on exhibits supplement the stuffed specimens (some of which are showing their age) and bring to life mammalian habitats, life cycles and evolution.

Less cuddly creatures get a look in too – 'Creepy Crawlies' is fun (even for confirmed arachnaphobes). In a highly interactive display visitors get to find answers to knotty questions like 'how do crabs mate?' or find out 'why a millipede is like a Swiss roll'. See where our many-legged friends make themselves at home in our homes and breathe a sigh of relief to discover some types of termite build their own high rise blocks.

Completed in 1977, the 'Human Biology' display contributed to the Museum being made Museum of the Year in 1980 – and it's still one of the best things here. After all, what could be more interesting than us? The human life cycle and the vital roles played by our

MUSEUMS - *WEST*

The Central Hall, The Natural History Museum

component parts are explored and, although highly educational, lots of exhibits are interactive to make the information accessible. Share a womb with a giant foetus (cheaper than a flotation tank!) or listen to a baby learning to speak. The 'Primates' and 'Our place in Evolution' displays put the whole process into a larger perspective. 'Origin of Species', an exhibition about Darwin, lets visitors play the 'natural selection' game on computer to put his theories into practice or learn how scientists could – shades of 'Jurassic Park' – bring an extinct species back to life.

From rainforest to desert, 'Ecology' looks at our environment, how it works and how mankind affects it. The giant 'leaf factory' shows how plants convert solar energy into food and a huge video wall follows the life cycle of water. Learn about webs, pyramids and the cycles of life – and recycle a rabbit.

The Earth Galleries can be reached from the Life Galleries but also have their own entrance on Exhibition Road if you want to explore here first. These galleries, the newest in the NHM, reflect the latest approach to museology: low on endless cases of sparsely-labelled specimens, high on participatory displays, sound effects and video monitors. With its six bronze statues depicting man's changing perceptions of the planet and its musical escalator leading up into a giant globe, the ground floor's 'Visions of the Earth' treads a fine line between the visionary and the naff. You can stop cringing when you get to the top of the escalator and the permanent displays like 'The Power Within' and 'The Restless Surface' get down to the nitty gritty. Stand under a volcano, 'experience' the 1995 Kobe earthquake or admire an extraordinary piece of lightning 'frozen' in the desert sand. Rocks, fossils, larva: the pieces which make up this jumbo jigsaw puzzle of a planet begin to fit together in the vivacious displays.

Covering some 4 billion years of Earth's history, the NHM certainly takes the long view and its Earth Galleries themselves are still evolving. Four more permanent displays are set to open, two in 1997 ('From the Beginning' and 'Earth's Treasures') and two the following year ('Earth Lab' and 'The Earth for Today and Tomorrow').

As you would expect from a museum of this size and status, an extensive programme of events and educational activities support the exhibits. Highlight tours of the museum depart every hour on the hour and there are daytime and evening courses for adults as well as field trips, both home and abroad. The Discovery Centre in the basement caters for 7-11 year olds – apart from the toads, more or less everything (including a lion) is a 'please touch!' exhibit. Activity sheets focus young minds, friendly explainers are on hand to guide youngsters and the atmosphere is welcoming. A café and restaurant will keep any hunger pangs at bay, for a price – the picnic area in the basement is only open at weekends and during school holidays. The museum's shops are pretty good too: if you have kids a selection of cuddly toys, games, kits and books mean you probably won't leave empty handed – more grown-up investments could include a whopping amethyst geode for just £1,950.

Pitshanger Manor & Gallery
- ⌨ *Mattock Lane, W5*
- ✆ *0181 567 1227*
- 🚌 *Transport: Ealing Broadway LU*
- 🕐 *Tues-Sat 10.00-17.00*
- 🎟 *Admission Free*
- ☕ *Café*
- ♿ *Wheelchair access*

Another example of Sir John Soane's inimitable architectural style (see also Bank of England Museum, p.8, Dulwich Picture Gallery, p.118, Soane's Museum, p.40), Pitshanger Manor now functions as an historic house, cultural centre and art gallery with a lively programme of events and exhibitions. The Victorian wing's extensive displays of Martinware pottery include a magnificent chimneypiece made for Buscot Park in Oxfordshire and the Manor's elegant interiors are being restored to their Regency style.

The Polish Institute and Sikorski Museum
- ⌨ *20 Princes Gate, SW7*
- ✆ *0171 589 9249*
- 🚌 *Transport: South Kensington LU, Knightsbridge LU*
- 🕐 *Mon-Fri 14.00-16.00; first Sat of every month 10.00-16.00*
- 🎟 *Admission free (donations appreciated)*

Containing over 10,000 items, this extensive collection of Polish militaria is a valuable resource for students of WWII. Friendly, knowledgeable volunteers (many of them veterans of the conflict) guide visitors around – offering a trenchantly Polish take on events and an interactive experience in the best possible sense of the word. Each branch of the Polish armed forces is represented with memorabilia ranging from battle colours, regimental badges and weapons to photos, documents and personal effects. Exhibits include a Nazi 'Enigma machine', a submarine map drawn from memory by the crew of the Eagle when their original charts were confiscated, and the uniform in which Poland's war-time leader, General Wladyslaw Sikorski died. Military paintings and prints line the walls, among them Feliks Topolski's lively portrait of Sikorski and a dramatic depiction of the Battle of Monte Cassino by Mezaj.

MUSEUMS - WEST

83

Royal College of Music: Department of Portraits and Performance History

🖾 *Prince Consort Road, SW7*
🕾 *0171 591 4340*
🚌 *Transport: South Kensington LU*
🕐 *Mon-Fri during term time by appointment*
🎨 *Admission Free (tours by arrangement)*
🕭 *Wheelchair access (by arrangement)*

The RCM's collection of portraits of musicians is the most comprehensive in the country, and is supplemented by around 500 prints and photographs of concert halls, opera houses and monuments, as well as the UK's largest archive of concert programmes.

Royal College of Music: Museum of Instruments

🖾 *Prince Consort Road, SW7*
🕾 *0171 591 4346*
🚌 *Transport: South Kensington LU*
🕐 *Weds in term time
   except January 14.00-16.30*
🎨 *Admission £1.20 (adults), £1 (concessions)*
🍽 *College cafeteria*
🕭 *Wheelchair access
   (by prior appointment, to ground floor)*

This world renowned collection of musical instruments dates from the C15th to the present day and consists of mainly European stringed, wind and keyboard instruments together with some Asian and African examples. Exhibits range from exotic-sounding creations like the clavichytherium right down to the humble recorder and, for those planning to build their own early instrument, full scale technical drawings of some instruments are for sale. Tours for groups can be made by appointment (extra charge).

Museum of Instruments

The Royal Hospital Chelsea Museum

🖾 *Royal Hospital Road, SW3*
🕾 *0171 730 0161*
🚌 *Transport: Sloane Square LU*
🕐 *Mon-Sat 10.00-12.00, 14.00-16.00,
   Sun (April-Sept) 14.00-16.00*
🎨 *Admission free*
🛍 *Shop*

Founded in 1682 by Charles II as a retreat for army veterans, the Royal Hospital fulfils the same function today and Chelsea Pensioners, in their anachronistic scarlet coats and tricorn hats, are a much loved sight along the King's Road. Pensioners' uniforms and medals are displayed in their small museum, as well as prints, paintings, photos and original documents illustrating the institution's history. Alongside the military memorabilia are a C17th chamberpot found during renovation work at the hospital and a button made from the oak tree in which Charles II hid. The Wellington Hall houses not only a vast canvas of the Battle of Waterloo but also an excellent shop with remarkably well-priced souvenirs (mugs for just £1.50, hand-painted model Pensioners £6). The Chapel and Great Hall are also open to visitors and, designed by Sir Christopher Wren, are well worth a look.

The Science Museum

🖳 *Exhibition Road, SW7*
🕾 *0171 838 8080 or 8008*
🚇 *Transport: South Kensington LU*
🕐 *Mon-Sun 10.00-18.00*
🖃 *Admission £5.95 (adults),*
   £3.20 (concessions) £27.50 (family);
   (free after 16.30)
🕸 *Shop*
🖵 *Cafés*

It seems museums nowadays just aren't complete without a snappy slogan by which to sell themselves. 'See inside for inspiration' is the line used by the Science Museum and – on the whole – this vast museum lives up to the adman's promise. And with over 10,000 exhibits arranged over 7 floors and in 40 galleries, it's probable a little perspiration will enter the equation too. Taking a broad view of historic and contemporary 'science', the museum encompasses technology, industry and medicine – everything from calculators to chemistry, dentistry to deep sea diving, Foucault's Pendulum to Stephenson's Rocket.

With a wealth of historic objects, the museum also prides itself on its interactive exhibits – over 2000 of them – most of which are geared towards children. If your kids favour the hands on approach start by visiting the 'Launch Pad' which offers a good introduction to the museum and, teeming with busy little boffins, has 50 experiments with jolly fairground ride names like 'Bucket Radio' and 'Giant Steelyard'. In the basement 'The Garden' is an exploration and discovery area for 3-6 year olds while aimed at 7-11 year olds 'Things' deals with everyday objects: how they are made and the effect they have on our lives. All these galleries are supervised by 'Explainers', green-shirted museum staff who are on hand to answer questions, guide experiments and stage educational performances.

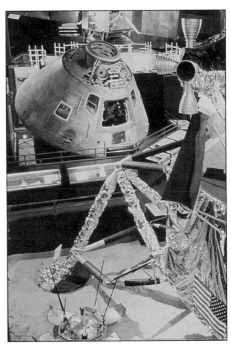

Exploration of Space, The Science Museum

Also in the basement and accessible to everyone, 'The secret life of the home' is an entertaining display charting man's struggle to conquer the domestic front. Given the technological wizardry on show elsewhere in the museum what's really amazing here is just how long it has taken humans to work out an effective way of doing the housework. The evolution of the humble toilet is shown in all its glory – culminating in a frank, funny presentation of how a modern flush loo works.

'The Exploration of Space' is a popular draw on the ground floor covering early rocketeers to men on the moon and modern satellite communications. A display on Arthur C. Clarke demonstrates the often uncanny affinities between science fiction and science fact. The huge Black Arrow satellite launcher runs practically the length of the gallery, while the original Apollo 10 Command Module looks rather miniature, and still bears its re-entry scars. There's also a look at life in space – complete with astronauts' undies and even a Coke can specially adapted for gravity free conditions.

The 1st floor is home to a funky new display 'The Challenge of Materials' which takes a new look at the manufacture, use and disposal of materials. The exhibits incorporate examples of art, architecture and fashion to challenge our perceptions. While visitors can boggle at unusual items like a steel bomber jacket, a rubber sofa or even a Bakelite coffin, hi-tech interactive exhibits let you to get to grips with how materials are developed and tested.

Contained within a vast hangar-like space, 'Flight' takes off on the 3rd floor. Flying machines of all descriptions hang from the ceiling like Airfix models – from papery biplanes to Britain's first jet plane – while ranged along one wall is a miscellany of gleaming aircraft engines. A high level walkway gives a bird's eye view of the planes which include several historic exhibits from the pioneering days of flight including the Vickers Vimy in which Alcock and Brown traversed the Atlantic. All these seem worlds away from the crowded skies of the late 20th century and the paraphernalia of routine jet travel: a cross section of a Boeing 747, an X-ray machine for luggage and an air traffic control suite bristling with lights, switches and split-second, life or death decisions. The 'Flight Lab' on the 3rd floor is a smallish interactive area which explains the principles of flight to 7 year olds and upwards, who can sample pedal-powered flight, or see aerodynamics in action in a mist tunnel. A flight simulator – used to train pilots on the cheap – costs extra and promises a rough ride even for those with cast iron stomachs.

On the same floor, older kids can literally take to the air - in the museum's own fully operational radio studio.

Produce your own programme or broadcast the museum's daily programme of demonstrations, workshops, tours and drama under the watchful (but not too intrusive) eye of an Explainer. 'On Air' also includes nifty interactive computers which enable visitors to become sound engineers and compile their own mixes. Great fun.

On a more serious note 'Health Matters' looks at modern healthcare, its documentary films supplemented by some grisly medical hardware like a 1950's iron lung. Displays about blood transfusion and the three bugbears of contemporary health – Aids, cancer and heart disease – seemed comprehensive enough. The top two floors of the museum, 'The Science and Art of Medicine', and 'Veterinary History' continue the gore with no end of wince-making exhibits: evil looking instruments, pickled bits and pieces and so on. Fans of hospital dramas should also enjoy the real life reconstructions of 'Glimpses of Medical History' – visit a 1905 pharmacy, go to a 1930's dentist or (if you've got the bottle) 'drop in' on a 1980's open heart operation.

This is just the tip of the iceberg, but don't discount the older galleries – just because there isn't a touchscreen computer in sight doesn't mean they aren't worth a good look around. While the newer galleries can get crowded and noisy, displays like 'Time Measurement' or 'Gas' remain havens of traditional museum hush. For quiet contemplation try 'Agriculture' on the 1st floor. Ponder the development of the plough and discover why Jethro Tull is an icon of farming, not rock music. 'Marine Engineering', 'Ships', 'Docks and Diving' on the 2nd floor are other enjoyable old-style galleries. Simple labels, although often out of date, let the objects speak for themselves and there's a stunning selection of model ships across the continents and through the ages.

If all that thinking makes you peckish, the museum has a couple of cafés and, while food and drink can be consumed on any uncarpeted areas, there are several picnic sites with seating. If you fancy a change of scenery, nearby Francofill at 1 Old Brompton Road serves French fast food (baguettes, Toulouse sausages and frites) with some style. The museum shop is well organised and stocked with gadgets and games from expensive gizmos like a fibre-optic flower lamp to cheapo gimmicks like kaleidoscope key rings. A Dillons bookshop sells an extensive range of relevant publications for all ages – activity books to heavy-weight tomes on 'the philosophy of science'.

There's a lot to see and, as with all big museums, a little pre-planning will ensure you get the most from your visit. Although there's no predetermined route for visitors to follow, if you have a whole day to spare the museum advises that you start at the top (galleries 4 and 5) and work down. For really eager egg heads, season tickets are available.

The Scout Association

- ⌨ *Baden-Powell House, Queen's Gate, SW7*
- ☏ *0171 584 7030*
- 🚌 *Transport: South Kensington LU, Gloucester Road LU*
- 🕐 *Daily 24 hours*
- ✹ *Admission free*
- 🛍 *Gift counter and Café*
- ♿ *Wheelchair access*

More along the lines of a foyer display than a 'museum', this permanent exhibition is nevertheless the only one in London to be open 24 hours a day. Recently refurbished, this cub-sized display narrates the story of the Scout Movement, and its founder Lord Baden-Powell. Exhibits include his army and scout uniforms, souvenirs of jamborees, some of the 'Freedom caskets' donated from around the world and excerpts from some of his reassuringly poor school reports.

MUSEUMS - WEST

Flight Exhibition, Science Museum

MUSEUMS - WEST

Victoria and Albert Museum

🖃 *South Kensington, SW7*
📞 *0171 938 8500*
📞 *0171 938 8441*
   (recorded information, general)
📞 *0171 938 8349 (recorded information,*
   current exhibitions)
📞 *0171 938 8676 (recorded information,*
   research facilities)
🚌 *South Kensington LU*
🕐 *Mon 12.00-17.50; Tues-Sun 10.00-17.50*
🍽 *Admission £5.00 (adults), £3.00 (OAP's),*
   £15.00 (season tickets), (free between
   16.30 and 17.50), (Free to under 18s,
   students, disabled and unwaged)
🛍 *Shops*
☕ *Café*
♿ *Wheelchair access (Exhibition Road entrance)*

I make no apologies for counting the V&A, the national museum for art and design, among my favourite museums. Founded in the great C19th era of improvement, it is still the sort of place which makes you feel better for having gone. It has long been cherished by artists, designers and scholars, for whom it acts as a massive source book to inspire innovation. The V&A's permanent collection spans several centuries and continents and includes textiles and fashions, musical instruments, jewellery, ceramics, glass and sculpture. Although known for its decorative art, the museum's Henry Cole Wing also contains an interesting assembly of paintings, prints, photography and sculpture.

A review of this size can't do justice to the V&A's diversity – and neither will a single visit. Little and often is the ideal approach, so if you can't take advantage of late afternoon free entrance, a season ticket is a sensible investment. Free guided tours (in English), depart from the Information Desk at the Cromwell Road entrance and last an hour. Those venturing in without a guide shouldn't be dismayed by the odd wrong turn: the V&A is

The Silver Galleries at The Victoria and Albert Museum

labyrinthine – even when armed with a floor plan – but getting lost is part of the fun and you are bound to stumble across something of interest on unplanned detours.

There are two sorts of gallery: those devoted to Materials and Techniques (like 'Ironwork' or 'Tapestries') and the Art and Design galleries (such as 'India' or 'Europe') in which objects are arranged by place or date to illustrate the cultural influences which formed them. The Far East Galleries contain the finest collections of contemporary Chinese and Japanese art outside the countries themselves. The magnificent newly refurbished Raphael Galleries fit into neither category. This austere, imposing space houses the seven enormous preparatory designs for tapestries commissioned for the Sistine Chapel. With their vivid colouring and serene composition, Raphael's 'cartoons' seem finer than the tapestries themselves.

In general, a trip to the V&A could save you an expensive jaunt to foreign climes. The two equally vast and impressive 'cast courts' are filled with plaster reproductions of famous sculpture and architecture. Here casts of the portal from Santiago de Compostella and Trajan's Column jostle for space with medieval knights and their ladies, Michelangelo's 'David' and several of his 'Unfinished Slaves' amongst others.

Real sculpture isn't in short supply either. There's a whole room devoted to Donatello and upstairs in the Henry Cole Wing there's a collection of Rodin's sculpture – including his notorious 'Age of Bronze'. The paintings in the HCW also repay closer study. Ignore the tatty hessian wallcovering and shabby carpets and look out for Frith's study for his painting 'Derby Day' and for the first ever painting by Degas to enter a British public collection, as well as works by the Barbizon School.

Italian Cast Courts

On the 6th floor of the wing, the paintings by Constable include a study for 'The Haywain' and some of his renowned cloud studies.

Other galleries are slicker. Touchscreen computers can be found in several galleries – such as the Samsung Gallery of Korean Art – and provide useful additional background information on the objects and the culture which formed them. The Glass Gallery has been completely redesigned in recent years and is now a glittering celebration of a fragile yet durable substance. Artifacts range from ancient glass perfume jars to elaborate candelabra, from humble drinking glasses to the latest glass goods from Murano. A dramatic glass staircase and balcony housing the study collection supplies a fairy tale piéce de résistance.

Visitors with a magpie sensibility should dip into the new Silver Galleries which have also been comprehensively overhauled. Somewhat bizarrely, this collection is housed in the former ceramics galleries whose elaborate interior bears the names of famous pottery centres from around the world. A 'Discovery Area' brings this gallery into the interactive age and visitors can make an impression by stamping the V&A hallmark, or play pot detective with a light box and some X-ray photos of silverware. A touch screen computer recounts the history of silver in England but the real stars of this gallery are the exhibits themselves which are beautifully evocative. As for the current ceramic galleries, to say they are extensive would be an understatement. Case after case charts mankind's love affair with clay: from ancient Egyptian artifacts, to Greek urns and Chinese funerary sculpture to ceramics decorated by Picasso, as well as the work of contemporary potters.

Dedicated followers of fashion can follow the changing shape of clothing from the C17th onwards in the Dress Gallery. The collection is beautifully displayed and goes right up to the present day, including designers like Paul Smith and Christian Lacroix, and finds wardrobe space for more ephemeral fashion accessories like spectacles, shoes and underwear. Style gurus will want to check out 'C20th Design' – a display which is both inspirational and aspirational. 'Design Now' provides an ever-changing showcase for the latest objects of desire. The C20th Galleries too have their fair share of must-haves – from Bauhaus to Bloomsbury – but also look at graphic design and typography.

In addition to the permanent collections, the V&A holds temporary exhibitions as well as a series of ever changing smaller displays. Visitors with children under 12, should keep their eyes peeled for the Activity Cart which is parked in one of the main ground floor galleries every Sunday and offers quizzes, trails and games (materials provided).

Once infamously advertised as 'an ace caff with quite a nice museum attached', the exact opposite is now true at the V&A. The basement restaurant is spacious and pleasant but food is on the pricey side – perhaps justifying the floor plan which now describes it as a 'restaurant'. With several miles of galleries, the V&A is thirsty work and on my visit I opted for the 'Café Espresso', which had sprung up in the gilded splendour of the Gamble Room. One of the museum's original refreshment rooms, this is a riotous confection of stained glass, gilt and cavorting cherubs. If ever there was an interior which demanded china cups and saucers and a bit of pizzazz, this is it and, frankly, the tiny cappuccino served in a plastic mug just wasn't up to scratch.

The museum shop however does live up to expectations and you may end up wishing you'd left your credit card at home. In addition to the usual postcards and posters, there is a good selection of art and design books and tasteful gifts. Jewellery, ceramics and textiles by contemporary British designers are on sale at the Crafts Council concession inside the shop and add a more cutting edge selection to the overall stock. A more child-oriented shop, featuring a smallish range of gifts, books and toys, can be found in the Henry Cole Wing.

Although the V&A's financial difficulties are no secret, the Lottery has enabled it to contemplate major capital projects. The next few years look set to see big changes at the museum – plans include a re-display of the entire suite of British galleries by 2001 and a controversial new building called 'the Spiral'.

Wilkinson Sword Museum

🗔 *Wilkinson Sword Centre,*
   19-21 Brunel Road, W3
🕾 *0181 749 1061*
🚌 *Transport: East Acton*
🕘 *Mon-Fri 8.00-15.00*
🍽 *Admission free (by prior appointment)*
🗇 *Sales point*
♿ *Wheelchair access*
   (advance notice required)

Mostly devoted to Wilkinson products, this museum (as you would expect from a company founded as a gunmakers in 1772) displays historic guns and swords as well as shaving equipment and, perhaps less predictably, an example of the Wilkinson TAC motorbike from 1910. It is sometimes possible to arrange tours of the on-site sword-making factory for small groups of visitors.

William Morris Society

🗔 *Kelmscott House, 26 Upper Mall, W6*
🕾 *0181 741 3735*
🚌 *Transport: Ravenscourt Park LU*
🕘 *Thurs and Sat 14.00-17.00*
🍽 *Admission free*
🗇 *Shop*

Only the basement and coach house of the riverside home of William Morris, are actually open to the public. Although by no means extensive, the displays reflect his dual role as doyen of the Arts & Crafts Movement and energetic pioneering socialist. Photographs of eminent early socialists in the coach house testify to its previous incarnation as the HQ of the Hammersmith Branch of the Socialist League while original decorative designs by Morris and exquisite embroideries by his daughter May offer a glimpse of the man's influential style.

William Morris Society

MUSEUMS - *WEST*

91

MUSEUMS - OUTSKIRTS

OUTSKIRTS

Brooking Collection of Architectural Detail

🏛 *University of Greenwich, Oakfield Lane, Dartford, DA1*
📞 *0181 331 9897*
🚌 *Transport: Dartford BR*
🕐 *Mon-Fri 9.00-17.00 (by appointment)*
🎫 *Admission free*
🍽 *Café (on campus)*
♿ *Wheelchair access*

An extraordinarily comprehensive reference collection of architectural features dating from 1525 to present day. Its fixtures and fittings, sourced from a huge variety of buildings, include over 700 complete or sectioned sash windows and material removed from Windsor Castle after the 1992 fire, as well as fireplaces, fanlights, staircases, rainwater heads, architrave mouldings, doors and wall post boxes.

The Cat Museum

🏛 *49 High Street, Harrow-on-the-Hill, HA1*
📞 *0181 422 1892*
🚌 *Transport: Harrow-on-the-Hill LU, South Harrow LU*
🕐 *Thurs-Sat 9.30-17.00*
🎫 *Admission Free*

The cat's whiskers for feline fans. Bitten by the collecting bug in the early 70's, proprietor Kathleen Mann now owns over 250 cat antique from all over the world, spanning from 1760 to 1940. English cats include a pair of smiley Staffordshire pottery moggies and pictures by famously loopy cat-painter Louis Wain. Kathleen's carefully labelled exhibits are arranged by country and housed in a tiny (space for only 2 visitors at a time) basement room.

Crossness Engines

🏛 *Thames Water Sewage Treatment Works, Belvedere Road, Thamesmead*
📞 *0181 303 6723 (contact)*
🚌 *Transport: Abbey Wood LU (2 miles)*
🕐 *Open: by appointment; 9.00-15.30 one Tuesday and one Sunday per month*
🎫 *Admission £2 (adults), £1.50 (children)*
🛍 *Shop*
♿ *Wheelchair access (limited)*

You name it – somehow, somewhere there's a museum about it. This Victorian sewage pumping station is no exception. Part of the vast sewer system which bought sanitation to the city in the last century, the works contain four massive beam engines, capable in their day of raising 6,237 litres of effluent at a stroke. And if you think that's impressive, the building itself is a rare example of a Grade I listed industrial building which features some exuberant decorative cast iron work. A museum of sanitation history is in the pipeline.

Forty Hall Museum

🏛 *Forty Hill, Enfield EN2*
📞 *0181 363 8196*
🚌 *Transport: Gordon Hill BR, Turkey Street BR*
🕐 *Thurs-Sun 11.00-17.00*
🎫 *Admission free*
🍽 *Café*
♿ *Wheelchair access*

Paintings and furniture are among the historic local exhibits in this museum, which is itself located in an imposing C17th pile, Forty Hall. The Raynton Room and Exhibition Gallery provide a venue for shows of local artists' work and the hall is surrounded by pleasant informal gardens and a 264 acre estate composed of parkland and a working farm.

Ham House

⌨ *Ham, Richmond, TW10*
☏ *0181 940 1950*
🚌 *Transport: Richmond BR*
🕐 *29 Mar-2 Nov: Mon-Wed 13.00-17.00,*
  Sat-Sun 12.00-17.00
🍴 *Admission £4.50, £12 (families)*
🛍 *Shop*
☕ *Cafés*

A C17th house on the banks of the River Thames. Much of the Duchess of Lauderdale's extravagant 1670's redecoration is still in place and its lush interiors include textiles, furniture and paintings. The garden features a wilderness and a cherry garden along with the all important licensed tea garden.

Hampton Court Palace

⌨ *Surrey KT8 9AU*
☏ *0171 316 4949 (advance tickets)*
☏ *0181 781 9500 (general information)*
🚌 *Transport: Hampton Court BR, Richmond*
  LU (then bus) or by river launch from
  Westminster, Richmond or Kingston
🕐 *March-Oct Tues-Sun 9.30-18.00,*
  Mon 10.15-18.00; Oct- March Tues-Sun
  9.30-16.30, Mon 10.15-16.30
🍴 *Admission £9.25 (adults), £7.00 (senior*
  citizens/students), £6.10 (under 16s),
  £27.65 (families), under 5's free; maze
  only (from 24th March) £2.10 (adults),
  £1.30 (children)
🛍 *Shops*
☕ *Cafés*

So vast is Henry VIII's Thameside palace that visitors are advised to allow 4 hours to do it justice. Its expansive red brick sprawl is a stunning example of Tudor (with later additions) architecture and its crenellated and turretted exterior everything you would expect from a royal palace. Inside it's not so bad either – from the state apartments and Renaissance picture gallery right down to the catering-

sized Tudor kitchens. Costumed guides and audio tours help interpret life in the royal household over the centuries and in the summer it's possible to meet the gardeners, housekeepers and other staff who keep Hampton Court ticking today. The gardens – all 60 acres of them – are as famous as the palace and include the newly restored C18th Privy Garden, the Great Fountain Garden and of course the Maze (although, depending on your navigational skills, you'll need to allow extra time to negotiate this).

Kew Bridge Steam Museum

⌨ *Green Dragon Lane, Brentford,*
  Middlesex TW8
☏ *0181 568 4757*
🚌 *Transport: Gunnersbury LU*
🕐 *Daily 11.00-17.00*
🍴 *Admission £2 (adults), £1 (concessions),*
  £5 (families) Weekend Admission
  (engines in steam) £3.25 (adults),
  £1.80 (concessions), £8.50 (families)
🛍 *Shop*
☕ *Café (open weekends only)*
♿ *Wheelchair access*

Opposing elements they may be but fire and water are inextricably linked in this magnificent Victorian pumping station. At least two of the museum's famous Cornish beam engines are 'in steam' every weekend, along with some of its other engines and 'Wendy', the station's locomotive, is put through her paces two weekends a month from April-Oct.

The newly opened 'Water for Life' gallery takes a close, sometimes microscopic, look at the history of London's water supply and doesn't fight shy of talking dirty. With the emphasis on interactivity and fun, visitors are invited to sift through a cess pit, control a sewer pipe robot and walk through part of the Thames Water Ring Main. Other exhibits include Roman toilet spoons (don't ask),

MUSEUMS - OUTSKIRTS

medieval ice skates and a modern sewage worker's protective clothing.

Large print site guides are available for visually impaired visitors and 'touch tours' can be arranged for groups. Special events are regularly held at weekends – past ones have included a festival of steam and young engineers discovery days.

Kingston Museum

- 🖃 *Wheatfield Way,*
  Kingston upon Thames, KT1
- 🕾 *0181 547 6738*
- 🚌 *Transport: Kingston BR*
- 🕘 *Daily 10.00-17.00 (closed Wed and Sun)*
- 🍴 *Admission free*
- 🛍 *Shop*
- ♿ *Wheelchair access*

As befits a royal borough, Kingston's museum is a pretty classy affair: a Grade II listed property, built with money donated by American benefactor Andrew Carnegie. In addition to the permanent and changing displays about Kingston's history, the museum has a fine collection of Martinware pottery and a zoopraxiscope donated by its inventor, photographic pioneer Eadweard Muybridge. The art gallery hosts national and local exhibitions.

Marble Hill House

- 🖃 *Richmond Road, Twickenham TW1*
- 🕾 *0181 892 5115*
- 🚌 *Transport: Richmond LU*
- 🕘 *22 Mar-31 Oct, daily 10.00-18.00*
  (dusk if earlier in Oct);
  1 Nov-31 Mar, Wed-Sun 10.00-16.00
- 🍴 *Admission £3 (adults), £2.30*
  (concessions), £1.50 (children),
  English Heritage Members free
- 🛍 *Shop*
- ☕ *Café*
- ♿ *Wheelchair access (ground floor)*

The serene symmetry and perfect proportions of its facade give Marble Hill House the appearance of a scaled up doll's house. In fact this elegant building, set by the Thames in 66 acres of parkland, was built by George II as a rural hideaway for his mistress. The Great Room is regally decorated with lavish gilding and the house contains early Georgian paintings and furniture along with the architectural paintings by Panini and a collection of chinoiserie. An exhibition, introductory film and audio tour are included in the admission price.

Merton Heritage Centre

- 🖃 *The Canons, Madeira Road, Mitcham, CR4*
- 🕾 *0181 640 9387*
- 🚌 *Transport: Mitcham BR;*
  Morden LU (then bus)
- 🕘 *Fri and Sat 10.00-17.00*
  (additional hours by appointment)
- 🍴 *Admission free*
- 🛍 *Shop*
- ♿ *Wheelchair access*

A programme of temporary exhibitions at this historic house tells the story of Merton and its inhabitants. With the emphasis on making local history accessible to all ages, the centre also organizes lectures, craft workshops and reminiscence sessions and exhibitions regularly feature hands on displays. The centre has a small sales point where visitors can buy local history publications and stationery and visitors can use the café facilities at the adjacent leisure centre.

Museum of Domestic Design & Architecture 1850-1950 –
incorporating The Silver Studio Collection

- 🏛 *Middlesex University, Bounds Green Road, N11*
- ☎ *0181 368 1299*
- 🚌 *Transport: Bounds Green LU, Bowes Park BR, New Southgate BR*
- 🕐 *Mon- Fri 10.00-16.00 (by appointment)*
- 🎟 *Admission Free*
- ☕ *Cafeteria*
- ♿ *Wheelchair Access*

Proving that 'design' isn't the exclusive preserve of the late C20th this extensive collection contains designs, wallpapers, textiles and ephemera by major British designers from 1850-1960.

Museum No. 1

- 🏛 *Royal Botanic Gardens, Kew, TW9*
- ☎ *0181 940 1171 (24 hr information)*
- 🚌 *Transport: Kew Garden LU*
- 🕐 *Open daily 9.30 onwards (telephone for closing time)*
- 🎟 *Admission included in entrance to Kew Gardens, £5.00 (adults), £3.50 (children)*
- 🛍 *Shop*
- ☕ *Café*
- ♿ *Wheelchair access*

It doesn't have to be lilac time to make a trip to Kew worthwhile - with over 30,000 different types of plants in the Gardens, it's always horticultural heaven. The newly restored Museum No.1 is an extra incentive for going. Its fun and interactive Plants + People exhibition shows how reliant humans are on plants for food, medicine, clothing and even personal hygiene! Intriguing exhibits include a cannibal fork and dish, a deadly bamboo blowpipe and gramophone needles made from cactus.

Museum of Richmond

- 🏛 *Old Town Hall, Whittaker Avenue, Richmond TW9*
- ☎ *0181 332 1141*
- 🚌 *Transport: Richmond LU*
- 🕐 *Tues-Sat 11.00-17.00, Sun (May-Oct only) 13.00-16.00*
- 🎟 *Admission £1 (adults), 50p (concessions); annual pass £3 (adults), £1.50 (concessions)*
- 🛍 *Shop*
- ♿ *Wheelchair access*

With a collection spanning from prehistoric times to present day, the museum celebrates Richmond's heritage as well as hosting regular temporary exhibitions.

The Museum of Rugby

- 🏛 *Rugby Football Union, Rugby Road, Twickenham, TW1*
- ☎ *0181 892 2000*
- 🚌 *Transport: Twickenham BR*
- 🕐 *Non Match days, Tues-Sat 10.30-17.00, Sun 14.00-17.00*
- 🎟 *Admission £2 (adults), £1.50 (concessions); joint price for museum and Twickenham*
- ☞ *Experience Tour £4 (adults), £2.50 (concessions) Match days, 11.00am to 1 hour prior to kick off (match ticket holders only)*
- 🛍 *Shop*
- ☕ *Café*
- ♿ *Wheelchair access*

Situated in the East Stand of Twickenham Stadium, this museum – newly opened in 1996 – charts the history of Rugby Football and its transformation from a free-for-all schoolboy game into an international sport. Many exhibits were donated by ex-rugby players and visiting teams – personal momentos include a mascot belonging to Robert Dibble who played for England no less than 19 times between 1906 and 1911. Visitors can

MUSEUMS - OUTSKIRTS

95

admire reconstructed period rooms, trophies, pictures and rugby ephemera, including cartoons of the comic side of the game by Fougasse. A film programme is shown at intervals during the day and for an extra charge a trip to the museum can be incorporated with a full tour of the stadium, entitled the 'Twickenham Experience'.

The Musical Museum

- ▥ *368 High Street, Brentford, TW8*
- ◐ *0181 560 8108*
- ▤ *Transport: Kew Bridge BR*
- ◷ *Sat and Sun 14.00-17.00 (April-Oct), Wed 14.00-16.00 (July and August)*
- ✇ *Admission £3.20 (adults), £2.50 (concessions)*
- ◈ *Shop*
- ♿ *Wheelchair access (advance notice appreciated)*

Automatic musical instruments are the stars of this show – from the lowly 'Tomasso Street' barrel piano to the swanky Steinway 'Duo-Art' grand which reproduces Gershwin's performance, and the multi-talented Popper 'Clarabella' Orchestrion. Visits take the form of a continuous demonstration in which instruments are explained and played – visitors should allow 90 minutes for a tour. Concerts are regularly held in the summer and the museum shop stocks a selection of music rolls, records and cassettes. Refreshments are available from the café at the nearby Watermans Arts Centre.

Old Speech Room Gallery, Harrow School

- ▥ *Church Hill, Harrow on the Hill, HA1*
- ◐ *0181 869 1205*
- ▤ *Transport: Harrow on the Hill LU*
- ◷ *Term-time daily (except Wed) 14.30-17.00*
- ✇ *Admission free*
- ◈ *Sales point*

The display includes Egyptian, Roman and Greek antiquities, and British watercolours and paintings.

Queen Charlotte's Cottage

- ▥ *Royal Botanical Gardens, Kew, TW9*
- ◐ *0181 332 5189*
- ▤ *Transport: Kew Gardens LU, Kew Bridge BR*
- ◷ *April-Sept, week-ends and Bank holidays 10.30-16.00*
- ✇ *Admission free with ticket to Royal Botanical Gardens*
- ☕ *Café*

Queen Charlotte's whimsical thatched cottage provided a scenic spot for the Hanoverian royal family's picnics as well as doubling up as the living quarters for their menagerie of exotic pets. Nearby Kew Palace – the favourite home of King George III and Queen Charlotte, and Britain's smallest palace – is being repaired and is due to open some time in 1999.

Riesco Gallery & Lifetimes Interactive Museum

▢ *Croydon Clocktower, Katharine Street, Croydon CR9*

☏ *0181 253 1030*

🚌 *Transport: East Croydon BR, West Croydon BR*

◔ *Mon-Sat 11.00-17.00, Sun and bank holidays 12.00-17.00*

🍵 *Admission £2 (adults), £1 (concessions), Admission free to Riesco Gallery*

🛍 *Shop*

☕ *Café*

♿ *Wheelchair access*

The Riesco Gallery displays a unique collection of Chinese pottery, dating from prehistory to the C19th, along with information about the people who once used these beautiful objects. Croydon through the decades is the subject of the Lifetimes Interactive Museum which explores the suburb's history from 1860 to the present day, based around the experiences and recollections of its residents. Both the gallery and museum also host temporary exhibitions.

The Royal Military School of Music

▢ *Kneller Hall, Kneller Road, Twickenham TW2*

☏ *0181 898 5533*

🚌 *Transport: Whitton BR, Twickenham BR*

◔ *By appointment only*

🍵 *Admission free*

☕ *Café*

♿ *Wheelchair access (limited)*

A private collection of musical instruments, uniforms, medals and other objects with a military connection.

Hampton Court Palace

MUSEUMS - OUTSKIRTS

GALLERIES - MAP

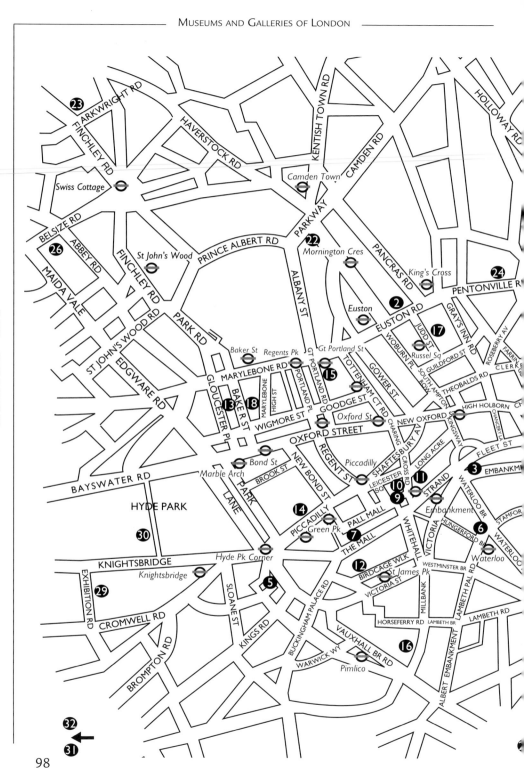

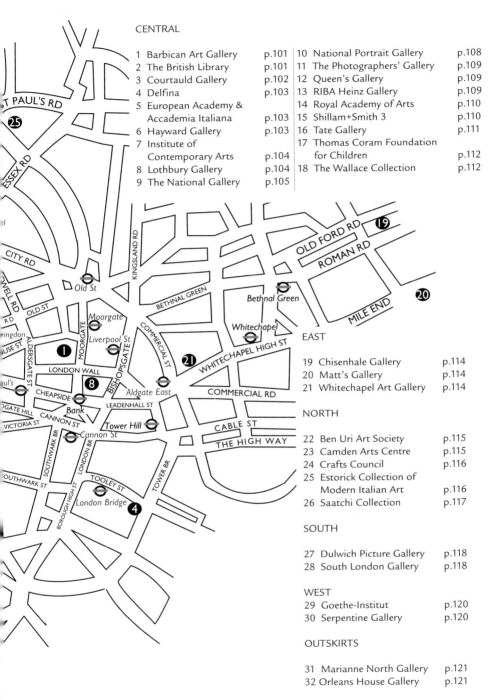

GALLERIES - MAP

GALLERIES

GALLERIES - CENTRAL

CENTRAL

Barbican Art Gallery

⌨ *Gallery Floor, Level 3, Barbican Centre, Silk Street, EC2*

☎ *0171 588 9023 (public information)*

🚍 *Transport: Barbican LU, Moorgate LU*

🕐 *Mon, Thur-Sat 10.00-18.45, Tues 10.00-17.45, Wed 10.00-19.45, Sun and Bank Hols 12.00-18.45*

🍽 *Admission £5, £3 (concessions, and after 17.00 Mon-Fri)*

🛍 *Shop*

☕ *Café*

♿ *Disabled access*

Set in the heart of the Barbican maze and comprising two gallery spaces, this venue hosts an eclectic range of temporary exhibitions – a recent retrospective of Belgium's expressionist painter James Ensor ran concurrently with an exhibition of works by photojournalist Don McCullin. In addition, the centre's concourse and foyer galleries hold free exhibitions of art and crafts.

The British Library

⌨ *Euston Road, NW1*

☎ *0171 412 7332 (Visitor Services Enquiries)*

🚍 *Transport: Euston LU, King's Cross/ St Pancras LU*

🕐 *Mon, Wed, Thurs and Fri 9.30-18.00, Tues 9.30-20.00, Sat 9.30-17.00, Sun 11.00-17.00*

🍽 *Admission Free*

🛍 *Shop*

☕ *Café/Restaurant*

♿ *Wheelchair access*

Nestling in the shadow of St Pancras, the new British Library is a remarkable achievement. Housing over 12 million books and a large daily influx of 'readers', this is now indisputably the UK's national library. But you don't have to be a book worm to enjoy it – as well as its superb research facilities, the library incorporates three glamourous new exhibition galleries and there are regular tours of the building (call the box office for information).

Featuring plenty of hands on exhibits, 'The Workshop of Words, Sound and Images' is an interactive introduction to the written and printed word, with an explanation of how sound is recorded thrown in for good measure. The workshop seems to be aimed at younger visitors, who can drop in on a medieval scribe, tap away at a 'Hot Metal' composing machine or have a go at desk top publishing. Not just a pretty exhibition space (although it is that as well), the workshop is used for regular demonstrations of bookcrafts such as calligraphy and bookbinding.

The five themed displays of books and manuscripts in 'The Pearson Gallery of Living Words' are a microcosm of the library's vast holdings. 'The Story of Writing' includes early forms of writing, along with ancient writing materials. 'Children Book's' features a reading area with specially selected new books, complementing the displays of kid's books through the ages. Richly illuminated manuscripts from a number of cultures are displayed in 'The Art of the Book' while the role of the written word in science is explored in 'The Scientific Record'. As you might expect in a brand new gallery, technology is much in evidence and the dynamic multimedia presentation is very different from the staid BL displays of old.

Both these exhibitions are a prelude to the permanent exhibition in The John Ritblat Gallery, 'Treasures of the British Library'. With books and manuscripts spanning some three thousand years, this is the place to pore over historic documents like Shakespeare's First Folio or to read through Captain Scott's last polar diary. Early maps offer insights in to our ancestors' world view and there is a

GALLERIES - CENTRAL

copious selection of sacred texts. The Literature section includes some rare manuscripts including Lewis Carroll's meticulously handwritten copy of 'Alice in Wonderland' and James Joyce's manuscript of 'Finnegan's Wake'. The Science section seems small but on the plus side includes a letter from Galileo to the artist Michelangelo discussing telescopes.

Unsurprisingly, given the priceless nature of the exhibits the lighting is kept low and the exhibits safely behind glass. An ingenious interactive 'Turning the Pages' gets around the restrictions of display. Its touchscreen computers lets you leaf through four of the library's most distinguished manuscripts.

For those with ambitions to build a library of their own, the bookshop on the ground floor is well stocked. Cards and literary gifts like 'quotable' t-shirts are available for those in a giving mood and the shop also sells limited edition hand-printed books. And if intellectual stimulation just isn't enough, the new library also boasts an in-house cafe and restaurant.

Courtauld Gallery

🏠 *Somerset House, Strand WC2*
📞 *0171 873 2526*
🚌 *Transport: Temple LU, Covent Garden LU*
🕐 *Mon-Sat 10.00-18.00; Sun 14.00-18.00*
🎫 *Admission £4 (free after 17.00)*
🛍 *Shop*
☕ *Café*
♿ *Wheelchair access*

Nb, the Courtauld Gallery will close on 31 August 1997 for refurbishment, and will reopen Autumn 1998.

Comprising a series of 11 different bequests, the Courtauld Gallery is that rare creature: a display of world-class art with the intimate feel of a private

collection. Its collections includes those of Austrian aristo Count Seilern and of Samuel Courtauld, textile impressario and founder of the eponymous neighbouring Institute of Art. Considerably less daunting than its surrounds (the austere Strand Block of Somerset House), the gallery also has the distinct advantage of being the ideal size to while away a morning or afternoon without having to resort to military-style route planning and clock watching.

The 1st floor galleries contain some of the finest C18th interiors in London (look up at the ceilings) and are home to a stunning collection of works by Rubens. Popularly known for his lardy ladies, what is striking here is the sheer emotional and physical force of works like 'The Descent from the Cross' and 'The Conversion of St. Paul'. In contrast 'Landscape by Moonlight' reveals Rubens in more tranquil mood whilst his affectionate portrait of 'The Family of Jan Breughel the Elder' shows the artist in yet another light. The gallery also contains the obligatory Canaletto – this one depicting Old Somerset House, a Thames-side scene imbued with an improbably Venetian flavour. Gainsborough's tender portrait of his wife is one of a group of C18th British portraits, whose civilised good taste is in contrast to the stark proto-expressionism of Daumier's depiction of Don Quixote and Sancho Panza in the next room.

For many the highlight of their visit will be the jaw-droppingly good collection of Impressionist and Post-Impressionist works in the upper galleries. It's difficult not to reduce this to a litany of famous names and iconic works: Van Gogh's 'Self Portrait with Bandaged Ear', Manet's enduringly enigmatic 'Bar at the Folies-Bergéres' and Gauguin's melancholic, mystical masterpieces 'Nevermore' and 'Te Rerioa' are just a few of the treasures. There's a whole wall devoted to Cézanne (including 'Man with a Pipe' and the sublime landscape 'Lac d'Annecy') while landscapes in a different vein can also be found by Monet, Renoir and Sisley. Compare the uptight pointillism of Seurat with the languid sensuality of Modigliani's 'Female Nude' which in turn points up the bawdy vivacity of Toulouse-Lautrec's 'Tête à Tête Supper', in which the viewer becomes the dinner date. The small display of English Post-Impressionist works looks rather half-hearted in comparison.

On the same floor but in a completely different vein are works dating from the C13th-16th by masters such as Fra Angelico (works which, somewhat mystifyingly share a gallery with a handsome piece of furniture that once served as Lord Iveagh's sock cupboard). Cranach's take on the Adam and Eve story repays closer inspection: Adam scratches his head, perplexed, while Eve (smiling knowingly) coyly hands him the Fruit of Knowledge.

Contemporary temptation at the Courtauld takes the more benign form of a shop and café – both of which are set to be 'reorganized' during the Gallery's year long refurbishment (hopefully to their advantage).

Delfina

- 50 Bermondsey Street, SE1
- 0171 357 6600
- Transport: London Bridge LU
- Mon-Fri 10.00-17.00, Sat-Sun 14.00-17.00

Part of the Delfina Studio Trust, this gallery mounts about five shows a year of contemporary, cutting edge British and International art; Martin Creed and Anya Gallaccio are among the artists who have shown here. The gallery's in-house restaurant means you don't have to venture far for refreshment.

European Academy & Accademia Italiana

- 8 Grosvenor Place, SW1
- 0171 235 0303
- Transport: Hyde Park Corner LU, Victoria LU
- Daily 10.00-18.00 (exhibitions closed Mondays)
- Shop
- Café

The two academies have joined forces to organise cultural and educational activities, including art exhibitions. Rather charmingly down-at-heel, their Grosvenor Place venue was, on my visit, hosting a display of works by Peter Griffin entitled 'Sealed by Fire (Images of Neruda)'. The café is pleasant, if somewhat smoky.

Hayward Gallery

- South Bank Centre, SE1
- 0171 921 0734 (SBC brochure request line)
- 0171 960 4242 (advance booking);
- Transport: Waterloo LU, Embankment LU
- Daily 10.00-18.00; late nights Tues and Wed until 20.00
- Admission £5 (adults), £3.50 (concessions)
- Shop
- Café
- Disabled Access (phone 0171 928 3144)

Squatting snugly at the core of the brutalist masterpiece/monstrosity that is the South Bank Centre, the Hayward is not the most alluring exhibition space in town. Nevertheless, it puts on a quality show: past ones have included 'Objects of Desire – the Modern Still Life', 'Rhapsodies in Black: The Harlem Renaissance' and the sublime 'Spellbound'. Books, postcards and exhibition merchandise are available in the gallery shop and the functional café is run by Aroma. If funds are low, soak up the sights and sounds of the free exhibitions and music staged in the foyer of the Royal Festival Hall next door.

GALLERIES - CENTRAL

103

The Institute of Contemporary Arts

Institute of Contemporary Arts

🖼 *The Mall, SW1*
🕐 *0171 930 3647 (box office)*
🚌 *Transport: Charing Cross LU,*
   Piccadilly Circus LU
🕐 *Mon 12.00-23.00, Tues-Sat 12.00-01.00,*
   Sun 12.00-23.00; Galleries:
   daily 12.00-21.00, Fri 12.00-21.00
🍴 *Admission ICA members free; £1.50 day*
   membership/
   £2.50 Sat, Sun during exhibitions,
   included with any ticket purchase
📖 *Bookshop,*
☕ *Café, Bar*
♿ *Limited wheelchair access*

For those who prefer their culture right slap bang up to the minute, the ICA provides a potent programme of art exhibitions, literary events, cinema and what their brochure refers to as 'live arts'.

You may have to take out day membership to get in but that's a small price to pay to visit what has been described (by no lesser personage than Bryan Ferry) as 'still one of the best clubs in London'. The recently opened New Media Centre has brought the 50 year old institute into the digital age and as well as acting as a space for virtual art works also offers access to a range of materials about the ICA programme. Their website is a useful place to browse for information (http://www.newmediacentre.com). Returning to the world of old technology, the bookshop does a nice line in trendy art tomes while the café offers more digestible fodder specialising in vegetarian and Italian food.

Lothbury Gallery

🖼 *41 Lothbury, EC2*
🕐 *0171 726 1642/1643*
🚌 *Transport: Bank LU*
🕐 *Mon-Fri 10.00-16.00 Admission free*
♿ *Wheelchair access*
   (ring bell at Lothbury entrance)

Housed in a former banking hall at the Nat West Group's Head Office, this gallery space opened in 1997 to provide a showcase for the Group's corporate art collection and a venue for changing exhibitions. Particularly strong on contemporary British art, the collection includes works by stalwarts such as Henry Moore and David Hockney as well as pieces by young bloods like Callum Innes and Mark Francis.

On a somewhat different note, a small room to one side of the gallery area houses 'Time Present and Time Past', a display of artifacts relating to the Group's banking activities. Its fiscal ephemera include a selection of prehistoric-looking early credit cards and a psychedelic cheque book cover from the 1960's.

The National Gallery

- 🏛 *Trafalgar Square, WC2*
- ☎ *0171 747 2885 (information line)*
  Web site: http://www.nationalgallery.org.uk
- 🚌 *Transport: Charing Cross LU,*
  Leicester Square LU, Embankment LU
- 🕐 *Mon-Sat 10.00-18.00, Wed 10.00-20.00,*
  Sun 12.00-18.00
- 🎟 *Admission free*
- 🛍 *Shops*
- 🍽 *Café and restaurant*
- ♿ *Wheelchair access*

Frequented by pigeons, rollerskaters and New Year revellers, Trafalgar Square is also a favourite haunt of art lovers, being home to Britain's National Gallery. A top-notch permanent collection of over 2,300 paintings spanning 700 years of Western European art history (from 1260-1900), the NG is the jewel in London's cultural crown. Some of the world's most famous paintings are housed here, among them van Gogh's 'Sunflowers', van Eyck's 'The Arnolfini Marriage', Leonardo da Vinci's 'Virgin of the Rocks' and the ever popular 'Haywain' by Constable.

The paintings (no wacky installations or performance art here – unless you count your fellow visitors) are arranged chronologically, the earliest paintings (1260-1510) being shown in the Sainsbury Wing, the newest and sleekest part of the Gallery. Designed by American architect Robert Venturi, it opened in 1991 and its calm, monochrome interior provides an ideally neutral backdrop for the gleaming gold leaf and vivid pigments of early Renaissance works like the Wilton Diptych. Christian iconography predominates but alongside the Annunciations, Nativities and Crucifixions

The Ambassadors' by Hans Holbein, The National Gallery

GALLERIES - CENTRAL

are beautifully observed portraits like Albrecht Dürer's 'The Painter's Father' and Giovanni Bellini's 'The Doge Leonardo Loredan'. Scenes from secular life include Uccello's 'The Battle of San Romano' whose composition reflects the artist's struggle with the laws of perspective while Botticelli's languid 'Venus and Mars' epitomises the Renaissance love affair with the classical past.

Moving back into the main building, the West Wing displays painting from 1510-1600 and includes works by Cranach, Bronzino, Titian and El Greco along with Michelangelo's unfinished 'Entombment' and Veronese's flamboyant set piece 'The Family of Darius before Alexander'. Holbein's newly restored 'The Ambassadors' is one of the highlights here, its ultra-realism managing to accommodate a smattering of symbolism and hidden meanings (stand to the side of the painting to view the death's head - an effect achieved by distorting perspective).

Northern European artists dominate the North Wing (painting from 1600-1700) - home to Vermeer's enigmatic 'Young Woman Standing at a Virginals'. The gallery's Rembrandts are concentrated here and, looking at his self-portraits, it's hard not to be moved by the artist's searing self-analysis and his descent from cocksure, successful thirty-something to dissolute, world weary 60 year old. Among the works by Southern European artists visitors can admire the curvaceous Rokeby Venus, Velasquez's C17th pin up, the darkly passionate fervour of Zurbarán's meditating St Francis or enjoy the gothic frisson of Caravaggio's 'Boy Bitten by a Lizard'.

The East Wing brings the collection up to 1900 - it's left to the Tate Gallery (p.111) to deal with the rest of the C20th. As part of an agreement to clarify the dividing line between the two institutions, the NG's C19th works have recently been augmented by a loan of over 50 paintings from the Tate, a haul which included works by Pissarro, Sisley, Gauguin and van Gogh. Hugely popular, the Impressionist and Post-Impressionist galleries always seem to be crowded - among the show-stoppers are a late Monet, 'The Water Lily Pond', Seurat's 'Bathers at Asnières', and Renoir's 'Parapluies'. Escape the crush in room 42, an intimate space hung with small, loosely painted sketches by the likes of Boudin, Corot and Degas. The wing's less fashionable galleries have treasures equally worth exploring - from frothy creations by Fragonard to landscapes by Constable and Turner to the Neo-Classicism of Ingres and David and the Romanticism of Delacroix.

Space restrictions ensure this review can only be a sketch - time restrictions will probably dictate how you will want to tackle the NG. Regular visitors can take advantage of free admission to drop in from time to time, savouring individual wings, rooms or even paintings. Those with limited time in the capital may likewise want to target particular areas of the collection or, armed with a floor plan, perhaps try an overview of the whole gallery. The Gallery Guide Soundtrack features a highlights tour of 30 masterpieces, but can also spoonfeed a complete guide with commentaries on individual rooms, paintings and artists as well as on subject matter and techniques. An alternative sound track guide, 'A Sense of Art' is available for visually impaired visitors and comes in a choice of 3 tours, complete with raised line diagrams and a large print text. Live guided tours run twice daily (11.30 & 14.30 Mon-Fri; 14.00 & 15.30 Sat) and are supported by an excellent programme of temporary exhibitions, short talks and lectures - ask for details at the desk on arrival or pick up a copy of National Gallery News.

Easy on the eye, the NG can be hard on the feet. Benches and squishy leather sofas offer some respite for weary art pilgrims but for hungry culture vultures the gallery has two in-house cafés. A Prêt à Manger outlet in the basement serves sandwiches, cakes and coffee in a vaguely frenetic atmosphere while the more civilized Brasserie in the Sainsbury Wing has waitress service, a mural by Paula Rego and a pretty reasonable set menu (2 courses £11.95, 3 courses £13.95).

Thwarted artistic ambitions can be consoled in the gallery's two shops with postcards, mugs, t-shirts and even slippers inspired by the works in the collection (although Cézanne would probably be turning in his grave to know that his famous 'directional brushstrokes' had inspired a range of crockery). The main shop in the Sainsbury Wing stocks a comprehensive range of art books.

The National Gallery

GALLERIES - CENTRAL

National Portrait Gallery

🖾 *St Martin's Place, WC2*

📞 *0171 306 0055*

🚌 *Transport: Leicester Square LU,*
   Charing Cross LU

🕐 *Mon-Sat 10.00-18.00, Sun 12.00-18.00*

🍴 *Admission free*
   (charge for some special exhibitions)

🛍 *Shop*

♿ *Wheelchair access (Orange Street entrance)*

Specialising in likenesses of famous British men and women through history, the NPG is perfect for people watching. With a collection of over 9,000 portraits in all media and more celebs than 'Hello!', here at least, it would be rude not to stare.

For a chronological view of Britannia's finest, start at the top floor. The collection opens with the Plantagenet and Tudor monarchs and includes Holbein's cartoon for his bullish portrait of Henry VIII. Wall labels clarify the complexities of the royal family tree, dramatically immortalised (if not entirely accurately) by one William Shakespeare – whose portrait by John Taylor was the first to be acquired by the gallery. As you work your way downstairs, encounter a succession of monarchs, mistresses, men of letters and public figures.

Founded in 1856, the gallery is a testament to the achievements and preoccupations of the C19th and, unsurprisingly, most of the first floor is dedicated to Queen Victoria's great and good. The 'Statesmen's Gallery' is filled with the busts and portraits of stern, bewhiskered dignitaries. Empire builders (a jaunty Lord Baden-Powell among them), artists and scientists populate the anterooms. Writers get a look in too: a tousle-haired Lord Tennyson and a trio of Brontës.

The Early C20th galleries have also been refurbished and are prefaced by Sir James Guthrie's enormous 'Some Statesmen of the Great War' out of which a centrally placed Winston Churchill stares knowingly. The 1918-1960 holdings have been suspended in a series of glass screens and are strong on the arts – T.S. Eliot, Delius, Kingsley Amis and a curiously Mrs Tiggywinkle-like Beatrix Potter among others. Changing displays of photographic portraits explore different aspects of the century such as the first women in parliament or children's writers.

On the ground floor, the Late C20th rooms reveal how the nature of fame has changed. Stand-up comedians, fashion designers, sports 'personalities' and ageing rock stars join the usual suspects from British public life. The Emmanuel Kaye Gallery attempts to redress the gallery's perceived bias towards the arts, with portraits of worthies from the worlds of science and technology.

The collection provides a gloriously voyeuristic tour through history, documenting changing attitudes and fashions more vividly than any history book. In an almost perverse reversal of the usual art gallery ethos, the celebrity of the subject holds sway over artistic merit – although that said there are works by luminaries like Gainsborough, Man Ray and David Hockney. Although photography was spurned by the gallery until the 1960's there's now a special room devoted to it, with a showcase for its extensive photographic collection. Temporary exhibitions supplement the permanent displays and visitors in search of a particular face in the crowd should note the gallery's reserve collection can be viewed by appointment. Information on the regular programme of events can be obtained from the Information Desk. The face of the NPG itself looks set to change: Lottery funding means additional gallery space, a basement lecture theatre and a rooftop restaurant are set to open in January 2000.

The Photographers' Gallery

- 🖃 *5 and 8 Great Newport Street, WC2*
- 🕾 *0171 831 1772*
- 🚌 *Transport: Leicester Square LU*
- 🕙 *Mon-Sat 11.00-18.00*
- 🐾 *Admission Free*
- 🗋 *Bookshop*
- 🖵 *Café*
- ♿ *Wheelchair Access (ground floor only)*

The first independent gallery in Britain to be devoted to photography, the Photographers' Gallery runs an invigorating exhibition programme, showcasing new talent as well as holding retrospectives of established names. Its Print Sales Room offers vintage, modern and contemporary prints for sale, while an extensive selection of photography publications can be found in the bookshop.

The Photographers' Gallery

Queen's Gallery

- 🖃 *Buckingham Palace, SW1*
- 🕾 *0171 799 2331 (recorded information)*
- 🚌 *Transport: Victoria LU, St James's Park LU, Green Park LU*
- 🕙 *Daily during exhibitions 9.30-16.30*
- 🐾 *Admission £4 (adults), £3 (over 60's), £2 (children)*
- 🕸 *Shop*

Temporary exhibitions of works from the Royal Collection (the largest private collection in the world). Past exhibitions have included drawings by Leonardo da Vinci and Michelangelo.

RIBA Heinz Gallery

- 🖃 *21 Portman Square, W1*
- 🕾 *0171 307 3628*
- 🚌 *Transport: Marble Arch, Bond Street, Baker Street LU*
- 🕙 *Mon-Fri 11.00-17.00; Sat 11.00-14.00*
- 🐾 *Admission free*

The UK's first architecture gallery, the diminutive Heinz Gallery hosts a varied programme of temporary exhibitions on architecture and design. In 1997, its silver jubilee, these included a look at the career of Portmeirion's whimsical 'architect-errant' Clough Williams-Ellis, an examination of architecture by women and the work of Professor Colin St John Wilson, architect of the controversial new British Library at St Pancras (see p.101).

The RIBA's collection of British architectural drawings – the largest in the world – is also housed at this address and open to the public (by appointment only; Tues-Thurs, closed August). Here you can contemplate carbuncles past and present and admire original designs by architectural masters like Inigo Jones and Robert Adam, as well as work by contemporary figures such as Quinlan Terry and Richard Rogers.

GALLERIES - CENTRAL

109

Royal Academy of Arts

- ⌨ *Burlington House, Piccadilly, W1*
- ☎ *0171 300 8000*
- ☎ *0171 300 5760/5761 (recorded information)*
- 🚌 *Transport: Piccadilly Circus LU, Green Park LU*
- 🕐 *Daily 10.00-18.00, late night opening Fri until 20.30 (Nov and Dec only)*
- ☕ *Admission £5.50 (adults), £4.50 (over 60s, registered disabled, UB40), £3.80 (NUS, ISIC members), £2.50 (12-18yrs), £1 (8-11yrs)*
- 🛍 *Shop*
- ☕ *Café*
- ♿ *Wheelchair Access*

Perhaps George III wasn't so mad – after all he founded this august institution (the oldest fine arts academy in Britain) in 1768. Today the Royal Academy is known for organising crowd-pleasing blockbuster exhibitions like 'Monet in the 90's' and 'the Glory of Venice', but it recently dipped a tentative toe into more challenging waters by hosting 'Sensation: Young British Artists from the Saatchi Collection' (see p.117). Punters flock to the RA's annual Summer Exhibition which, with over 1000 exhibits, is the world's largest open art exhibition. Offering a mind-bogglingly diffuse vision of contemporary British art, the show attracts as much critical disdain as it does popular acclaim. A bronze statue of Sir Joshua Reynolds, the Academy's first president, greets visitors as they enter the courtyard of Burlington House – works by Reynolds and Academicians, both dead and alive, make up much of the Permanent Collection; a small selection hangs in the Private Rooms and can be seen as part of a free guided tour (Tues-Fri 13.00).

Royal Academy

Shillam+Smith 3

- ⌨ *122 Great Titchfield Street, W1*
- ☎ *0171 637 0057*
- 🚌 *Transport: Oxford Street LU, Goodge Street LU, Great Portland Street LU*
- 🕐 *Mon-Fri 9.00-18.00 and by appointment*
- ☕ *Admission Free*

Located in the same building as Shillam+Smith Architects (specialists in urban regeneration), the gallery is run on a non-profit making basis and is dedicated to showing contemporary work of all types. Since opening in 1996, it has exhibited work by both young and established artists from Britain, Europe and the Americas.

GALLERIES - CENTRAL

Tate Gallery

- *Millbank, SW1*
- *0171 887 8000*
- *0171 887 8008 (information)*
- *Transport: Pimlico LU*
- *Daily 10.00-17.50*
- *Admission Free*
  (except for major loan exhibitions)
- *Shop*
- *Café, Restaurant*
- *Disabled Access (via the Clore Gallery)*

Along with its sibling sites in Liverpool and St Ives, the Tate Gallery at Millbank houses the national collections of British and modern art. Originating with sugar baron Henry Tate's bequest of C19th British pictures, the gallery's holdings now comprise over 4,000 paintings and more than 1,000 sculptures, while the Turner Bequest (in the Clore Gallery) alone contains some 38,000 works on paper. The introduction of regularly changing displays upset some diehard gallery-goers but has enabled more of the collection than ever before to be shown in the limited space of the Millbank building. Unfortunately, it also makes it impossible to predict exactly what visitors will see on a visit. To give you some idea of what to expect, in 1997 (the Tate's centenary year), Mondrian and Ellsworth Kelly were the subject of two major loan exhibitions, and displays from the permanent collection included Jackson Pollock, William Hogarth, the Pre-Raphaelites, Georg Baselitz, Constable and his contemporaries Rodin, Degas, Giacometti and Dubuffet.

Free lunchtime lectures are held in the auditorium and guided tours are given daily; for those who prefer to go it alone, an audio guide to the collection can be hired for £2 (£1.50 concessions). The gallery shop is well stocked with books and merchandise but the café is disappointing, offering its captive audience overpriced food in a charmless, subterranean setting.

The much trumpeted opening of the Tate Gallery of Modern Art at Bankside in Spring 2000 is set to change the shape of the Tate for ever. An audacious millennial scheme will transform the vast spaces of Sir Giles Gilbert Scott's power station into a major museum for the art of the twentieth and twenty-first centuries, while in the following year the Millbank site will be relaunched as the Tate Gallery of British Art, with displays of native art from the Renaissance to the present day. Both British and Modern collections will continue to be displayed at Millbank while this revolution takes place, although some of its galleries will be closed for the duration.

The Tate Gallery

GALLERIES - CENTRAL

111

GALLERIES - CENTRAL

Thomas Coram
Foundation for Children

- 🏛 *40 Brunswick Square, WC1*
- 🕐 *0171 278 2424*
- 🚌 *Transport: Russell Square LU*
- 🕐 *Open by appointment*
- 🎫 *Admission £2 (£1 concessions)*
- ♿ *Wheelchair access*

William Hogarth (see p.76) got the ball of this art collection rolling in 1740 by presenting the Foundling Hospital with his portrait of philanthropist Thomas Coram. Other artists of the day followed suit and the cream of the collection includes paintings by the likes of Ramsay, Reynolds and Gainsborough and sculpture by Roubiliac and Rysbrack. Established in an age when art was seen as a force for moral improvement, the collection was intended to benefit the public and formed a precursor of the Royal Academy (see p.116). An art collection in the broadest sense, it also embraces music, architecture and the decorative arts of cabinet-making, clock-making, plasterwork and wood-carving.

Captain Thomas Coram by Hogarth (1740)

The Wallace Collection

- 🏛 *Hertford House, Manchester Square, W1*
- 🕐 *0171 935 0687*
- 🚌 *Transport: Bond Street LU*
- 🕐 *Mon-Sat 10.00-17.00, Sun 14.00-17.00 (Sun, Spring and Summer 11.00-17.00)*
- 🎫 *Admission free*
- 🛍 *Shop*
- ♿ *Wheelchair access*

Bequeathed to the nation in 1897, the Wallace Collection is one of London's gems. Housed in a sumptuous Italianate palazzo in a leafy Marylebone square, it's chock full of works of art acquired in the C19th by the aristocratic Hertford family. It's a cornucopia for connoisseurs, but the casual visitor will enjoy the collection's ambience as much its artifacts: an old-fashioned aura of discreet luxury, with antique clocks ticking quietly in gracious rooms, and friendly, helpful room stewards.

Many famous paintings reside here – Frans Hals 'The Laughing Cavalier', Poussin's 'A Dance to the Music of Time' and Fragonard's deliciously frothy 'The Swing' among them. Hertford House is also home to top notch old master paintings by Titian, Rubens, Murillo and Canaletto, and portraits by Gainsborough and Reynolds. Some of the subject matter is on the racy side – there's a wonderfully louche portrait of Lady Hamilton, Nelson's squeeze, reclining on a leopardskin in a state of semi undress, as well as a clutch of risqué Dutch genre paintings like Jan Steyn's 'The Lute Player'.

Four galleries are given over to baronial-style displays of European and Oriental arms and armour, some of it incredibly elaborate. Tucked away in the corner of one case is a leather pouch containing some clay pipes and a tobacco stopper – allegedly once owned by keen smoker Sir Walter Raleigh. More feminine sensibilities should revel in the extensive collection of Sévres porcelain. Newly displayed in glittering stainless steel and mirrored cases, the jewel-like colours of these pieces shine out with startling intensity: sugar pink, turquoise, royal blue and bright green. Among the goodies are two lavish ice cream coolers from the 'Catherine the Great' service – one of the most expensive ever produced in Europe.

Other displays include gold boxes, C18th French furniture, Renaissance bronzes, medieval manuscripts and Majolica pottery. Daily tours, both general and more specialised, help the visitor make the most of this diversity – given by Wallace Collection staff and other art experts, these are free of charge and last about an hour.

The shop on the ground floor has an upmarket feel to it: scholarly catalogues don't come cheap, but small booklets about the collection only cost £2.50. As well as the usual posters and postcards, there's an interesting range of gifts inspired by the collection – colourful 'Sévres' tin picnic plates should bring a certain finesse to al-fresco dining at £4.99 each, and also on offer are pewter helmet paperweights at £13.50, and silk scarves at £25.

The completion of the Wallace Collection's ambitious Centenary Project in June 2000 will not only see the opening of four new galleries, a lecture theatre and other educational/research facilities in the basement, a new sculpture garden and café in the courtyard but better facilities for disabled visitors and parents with young children. Until then, visitors needing a food fix should try the excellent Tropical Café on Chiltern Street, which serves delicious, well priced Brazilian food in friendly surroundings.

Lady Hamilton from The Wallace Collection

GALLERIES - CENTRAL

GALLERIES - EAST

EAST

Chisenhale Gallery

- Chisenhale Road, E3
- 0181 981 4518
- Transport: Bethnal Green LU, Mile End LU
- Wed-Sun 13.00-18.00
- Admission Free

New work, specially commissioned by the gallery from selected young artists.

Matt's Gallery

Matt's Gallery

- 42-44 Copperfield Road, E3
- 0181 983 1771
- Transport: Mile End LU
- Wed-Sun 12.00-18.00
- Admission Free

Uniquely in Britain, this publicly funded art gallery also represents artists – its 'stable' of contemporary young artists includes Richard Wilson and Lucy Gunning. All the exhibited work, be it painting, video installation or sculpture, is commissioned specially for the gallery space.

Whitechapel Art Gallery

- Whitechapel High Street, E1
- 0171 522-7888
- 0171 522 7878 (recorded information)
- Transport: Aldgate East LU
- Tues-Sun 11.00-17.00
- Admission Free
  (1 paying exhibition per year)
- Bookshop
- Café
- Disabled Access

Now one of Britain's leading venues for exhibitions of modern and contemporary art, the Whitechapel opened in 1901 with the aim of bringing major artworks to London's East End. It's certainly achieved that goal with distinction – Picasso's 'Guernica' was shown here in 1939 and in the post-war period the Whitechapel showcased trailblazing artists such as Jackson Pollock and David Hockney. More recently, video artist Bill Viola has exhibited here while the 'Lines from Brazil' show took the long view by following in the footsteps of exhibitions of Hispanic art held by the gallery as long ago as 1969. The regularly changing programme of exhibitions includes a biennial open show of works by artists living and working locally.

NORTH

Ben Uri Art Society

- 🖃 *126 Albert Street, NW1*
- ☎ *0171 482 1234*
- 🚌 *Transport: Camden Town LU*
- 🕐 *Mon-Thurs 10.00-16.00, selected Suns 14.00-17.00 (Closed for Jewish Festivals)*
- 🍽 *Admission free*

The Society was founded in 1915 and is dedicated to promoting Jewish art as a fundamental part of the Jewish heritage. At present working to establish a Jewish Arts and Cultural Centre in London, the society is in temporary accommodation and its programme of contemporary art exhibitions is being staged in a number of different venues. Its permanent collection of over 800 works by artists such as Frank Auerbach, David Bomberg and R. B. Kitaj can be viewed by appointment.

Camden Arts Centre

- 🖃 *Arkwright Road (corner of Finchley Road), NW3*
- ☎ *0171 435 2643/0171 435 5224*
- 🚌 *Transport: Finchley Road LU, Hampstead LU*
- 🕐 *Tues-Thurs 11.00-19.00, Fri-Sun 11.00-17.30*
- 🍽 *Admission Free*
- 📕 *Bookshop*
- ♿ *Limited disabled access (advance notification required)*

A contemporary art venue with a 'roll up your sleeves and get stuck in' approach to the visual arts. Visitors are encouraged to get involved in the centre's integrated programme of exhibitions and educational projects, artist-led workshops and debates. With a policy of showing both established and emerging artists. The bookshop stocks art books and catalogues as well as a range of limited edition publications.

The Sabbath Rest by Samuel Hirszenberg from the Ben Uri Art Society

GALLERIES - NORTH

Glass Work by Ray Flavell, Crafts Council

Crafts Council

🖃 *44a Pentonville Road, N1*
📞 *0171 278 7700*
🚌 *Transport: Angel LU*
🕐 *Tues-Sat 11.00-18.00, Sun 14.00-18.00*
🍽 *Admission Free*
🗃 *Shop*
☕ *Café*
♿ *Wheelchair Access*

Shrugging off the folksy image of crafts, the Crafts Council HQ provides a sleek and stylish – all white walls and pale wood floors – venue for a diversity of applied art exhibitions. Jewellery, furniture, ceramics, and even spectacles have been the subject of recent exhibitions at what is the national centre for the crafts. The shop is full of similarly tempting goodies – although the price tags reflect the handmade, designer nature of the stock. Although there's not a corndolly in sight, the carefully-honed slickness stops at the café upstairs, which serves tasty wholesome fare in a reassuringly homespun atmosphere.

Estorick Collection of Modern Italian Art

🖃 *Northampton Lodge,*
39a Canonbury Square, N1
📞 *0171 704 9522*
🚌 *Transport: Highbury and Islington LU*
🕐 *Tues-Sat 11.00-18.00*
🍽 *Admission £2.50 (£1.50 concessions)*
Free on Tuesday
🗃 *Shop*
☕ *Café*
♿ *Wheelchair access*
(except first floor galleries and library)

Works by Futurist artists Balla, Severini and Boccioni are at the heart of this superb private art collection, amassed by Eric and Salome Estorick after WWII. Opened in January 1998 and housed in a specially refurbished Georgian building, the collection has the distinction of being Britain's first museum devoted to modern Italian art. Other major C20th Italian artists represented are hallucinatory painter Giorgio de Chirico, Giorgio Morandi and master of the anorexic portrait, Amedeo Modigliani. Bronzes by

Marino Marini and Giacomo Manzù are among the sculptures on show. Long term loans from other private collections will supplement the permanent displays in a series of regularly changing exhibitions.

Saatchi Collection

- 98a Boundary Road, NW8
- 0171 624 8299 (information line)
- Transport: St John's Wood LU, Swiss Cottage LU, Kilburn LU
- Thurs-Sun 12.00-18.00
- Admission £4, £2 (concessions) Free on Thurs
- Disabled access (ring in advance)

Advertising supremo Charles Saatchi doesn't miss a trick when it comes to buying art. His collection of contemporary paintings, sculptures and installations runs to over 1,000 items and contains some of the most high profile art of recent years. Damien Hirst's shark (or should that be hype?) in formaldehyde, Jake and Dinos Chapman's 'Tragic Anatomies', Rachel Whiteread's 'Ghost' and Marc Quinn's self-portrait made from frozen blood are among the controversial sculptures. If some of these sound a bit too much like the Hunterian Museum for comfort (see p.33), the collection also holds painterly works by Fiona Rae and Gary Hume.

Although the focus is on the art world's current darlings, the YBA's (Young British Artists), past exhibitions have showcased contemporary German and American art while guest exhibitions at the gallery have included 'Out of Africa', a show of contemporary African Art, and Vogue's photographic exhibition 'A Positive View'. It may not be everyone's idea of art, but the collection, housed in 30,000 airy square feet of former warehouse, has attracted over a million visitors since opening to the public in 1985.

The Saatchi Collection

SOUTH

Dulwich Picture Gallery

🖼 *College Road, SE21*
📞 *0181 693 5254*
🚌 *Transport: North Dulwich BR*
🕐 *Tues-Fri 10.00-17.00; Sat 11.00-17.00;*
   Sun 14.00-17.00
🍽 *Admission £3 (adults), £1.50 (concessions)*
🛍 *Shop*
♿ *Wheelchair access*

Tucked away in a pleasant backwater of London, the DPG's small but perfectly formed display of old masters is a delight for art lovers. Arranged by country, the display of pictures has been described as a progression from the beer drinkers (Northern European artists) to the wine drinkers (the French, Spanish and Italian schools). A quick glance around the walls reveals a fair smattering of milk drinkers too – as in Rubens' voluptuous 'Venus, Mars, Cupid' or Poussin's scene 'The Nurture of Jupiter'.

Rembrandt's 'Girl leaning on a window sill' is perhaps the gallery's most famous work and in days gone by was the one most copied by art students – an honour which today falls to Poussin (who is represented in the gallery by nine superlative paintings). The gallery is full of familiar faces and names – Murillo's ever serene 'Flower Girl', Joshua Reynold's bespectacled self-portrait and Gainsborough's double portrait of those beautiful chanteuses, the Linley sisters. A larger than life 'John the Baptist in the Wilderness' by Guido Reni oversees the Italian room where Sebastiano Ricci's action-packed canvas 'The Fall of the Rebel Angels' should be enough to keep viewers on the straight and narrow for a while.

Entertaining but concise wall labels accompany the paintings and there's also a useful map showing the highlights of the collection. The gallery's distinctive building is as noteworthy as its contents – built by Sir John Soane (see p.40), it is England's oldest public gallery as well as being the inspiration behind Sir Giles Gilbert Scott's design for the classic red telephone box of the 1920's. The gallery holds about three temporary exhibitions a year and has recently opened up its grounds as a venue for sculpture exhibitions. If funding from the Lottery is forthcoming, the site will be closed from 1999 to early 2000 while improvements are made to the gallery and its facilities. Let's hope that these changes won't spoil the friendly, old-fashioned ambience which is a much loved feature of the gallery.

South London Gallery

🖼 *65 Peckham Road, SE5*
📞 *0171 703 6120*
🚌 *Transport: Elephant and Castle LU*
   (then bus); Oval LU (then bus)
🕐 *Tues, Wed, Fri 11.00-18.00; Thurs 11.00-*
   19.00, Sat and Sun 14.00-18.00
🍽 *Admission free*
♿ *Difficult disabled access*

Founded over a century ago to bring the best in contemporary art to the 'working man of Peckham', the South London Gallery still stages temporary exhibitions of hip, happening artists like Tracey Emin and Georgina Starr. Its collection of Victorian and later British art includes work by Leighton, Millais and Spencer held in storage but was recently the inspiration for an exhibition by students from Goldsmiths College.

Dulwich Picture Gallery

GALLERIES - *SOUTH*

WEST

Goethe-Institut

- 50 Princes Gate, Exhibition Road, SW7
- 0171 411 3400
- Transport: South Kensington LU
- Opening hours vary;
- Admission free
- Café (Mon-Thur 9.30-21.00, Fri 9.30-14.00, 17.00-20.30, Sat 9.00-12.30)

London's German cultural institute is a venue for temporary art exhibitions as well as for film screenings and languages courses. A recent series of shows has explored 'Conceptual Art in Germany since 1968', culminating in Marcel Odenbach's 'Vicious dogs' video installation.

Serpentine Gallery

- Kensington Gardens, W2
- 0171 402 6075/0171 723 9072
- Transport: Lancaster Gate LU, South Kensington LU
- Daily 10.00-18.00
- Admission Free
- Bookshop
- Wheelchair Access

Art and nature combine perfectly at this publicly funded art gallery. Set in the pastoral C18th landscape of the Royal Park, and housed in a former 1930's tea pavilion, the Serpentine provides an informal, relaxed location for viewing exhibitions of modern and contemporary art – the gallery's unique atmosphere and abundant natural light have been praised by artists and critic alike. Often challenging and controversial, past shows have included Jean-Michael Basquiat and Man Ray. The gallery reopened early in 1998, enhanced by a £4 million renovation. New lavatories, nappy-changing facilities, and an enlarged bookshop are among the new features.

The Serpentine Gallery

OUTSKIRTS

Orleans House Gallery

Marianne North Gallery

🏠 *Royal Botanic Gardens, Kew, TW9*

📞 *0181 332 5621*

🚌 *Transport: Kew Gardens LU*

🕐 *Open daily 9.30 onwards*
   (telephone for closing time)

🍴 *Admission (includes entrance to Kew*
   Gardens) £5.00 (adults), £3.50 (Children)

🛍 *Shop*

☕ *Café*

Marianne North was a Victorian artist who specialised in painting flowers with remarkable single-mindedness. An indefatigable traveller, she voyaged across the world to paint plants in their natural habitat, visiting Australia and New Zealand at the suggestion of Charles Darwin. Although she lacked any formal art training, Miss North was a fast worker and today some 832 of her distinctive oil paintings can be seen in the purpose built gallery she gave to the Botanic Gardens.

Orleans House Gallery

🏠 *Riverside, Twickenham, TW1*

📞 *0181 892 0221*

🚌 *Transport: St Margarets BR, Richmond LU*

🕐 *Tues-Sat 13.00-16.30 (17.30 April-Oct),*
   Sun 14.00-16.30 (17.30 April-Oct)

🍴 *Admission £1 (adults), children free*

🛍 *Small shop*

♿ *Wheelchair access*
   (to ground floor and Octagon Room)

A vibrant and varied programme of events means a new exhibition opens here every six weeks or so. The work of local artists, designers and photographers, and of young curators is showcased here, as well as items from the gallery's collection of Old Masters. The gallery is located in the remains of a royal residence, but if that doesn't cut any ice with the kids, the activity packs and half term and Sunday workshop days should do the trick. If you run out of things to do on this side of the river, you can always hop on a ferry to Ham House (see p.93) on the other bank.

GALLERIES - OUTSKIRTS

COMMERCIAL GALLERIES

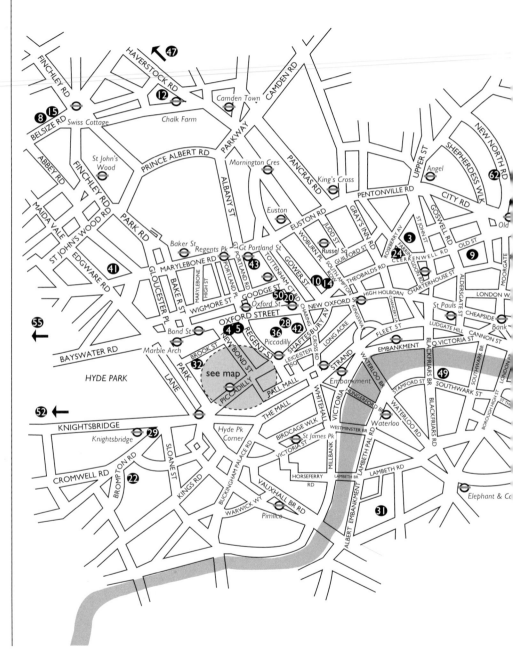

MAP GALLERIES -COMMERCIAL

INTRODUCTION

As befits one of the world's pre-eminent art capitals, London is positively brimming over with commercial galleries. In fact there are literally hundreds of these 'art shops', catering for all tastes and pockets but, given the space restrictions of this guide and the somewhat fickle nature of the art trade, this section doesn't attempt to provide an exhaustive listing. Rather, its selection aims to give some idea of the range of galleries in London and to act as a springboard for independent exploration.

Art lovers planning to do some serious gallery-going should look out for 'Galleries', a monthly magazine with gossipy art world editorial, reviews and reasonably comprehensive listings of current shows. In a similar vein, the more specialised bimonthly listings leaflet 'New Exhibitions of Contemporary Art' gives the lowdown on where to sample the latest trends in art. Both publications come complete with maps and are available free of charge at participating galleries.

Once Cork Street was shorthand for *the* place to see the best in contemporary art but, although 'the street' is still home to some prestigious and long-established galleries, top quality, cutting edge art emporia can now be found all over London. In recent years Hackney has reinvented itself as the city's artist quarter and is chock-a-block with studios and galleries (see freebie leaflet 'The Hidden Art of Hackney', or ring 0171 729 3301 for details), while the forthcoming Tate Gallery at Bankside looks set to transform Southwark into a new focal point for contemporary and modern art. Although Bond Street and St James remain the heartland of the most exclusive dealers (in both Old Masters and modern art), really dedicated gallery goers now have to venture well beyond the cosseted confines of W1 to keep up to date. But the extra travelling is well worth the effort – London's gallery scene has never been so diverse, so vibrant, or so innovative.

Of course there's no denying that, with their chic, white-walled interiors, telephone number price tags and well bred staff, some galleries can appear intimidating. Look beyond the classy accoutrements though and the bottom line is that galleries are essentially shops selling a commodity, and remember that no retailer ever made money by turning people away. There's no need to brazen it out, galleries are just as much a magnet for scruffy art students as they are for Gucci-clad collectors. (Incidentally, if you're not "just looking" but in the market for a little something to put over the mantlepiece, do bear in mind that most galleries, no matter how plush, carry stock at a wide range of prices and that it's always worth asking a dealer for their 'best price').

In the context of this guide though, what's more pertinent is that commercial galleries can often be the place to see museum-quality art work. Many galleries put on a new exhibition every 4-6 weeks (a much faster turnaround than bureaucracy-bound museums) with particularly important shows being accompanied by glossy, sometimes scholarly, catalogues, and attracting serious media coverage. As so-called public art galleries are increasingly obliged to charge for admission, perhaps it's not so far fetched to think of commercial galleries as the new museums, fulfilling an egalitarian, even educational, role – after all they're open to the public, are free of charge and generally far less crowded than the congested blockbuster shows put on with increasing frequency by cash-strapped museums. Perhaps culture and capitalism aren't such strange bedfellows after all...

Agnew's

Agnew's

- 🖼 43 Old Bond Street and 3 Albemarle Street, W1
- 🕾 0171 629 6176
- 🚌 Transport: Green Park LU, Piccadilly Circus LU
- 🕐 Mon-Fri 9.30-17.30, Thurs until 18.30

The gallery is known for its stock of Old Masters, but it also deals in English paintings, drawings and watercolours as well as C20th and contemporary British work.

Alan Cristea Gallery

- 🖼 31 Cork Street, W1
- 🕾 0171 439 1866
- 🚌 Transport: Green Park LU, Piccadilly Circus LU
- 🕐 Mon-Fri 10.00-17.30, Sat 10.00-13.00

Formerly Waddington Graphics, this gallery specialises in prints by an international range of artists.

The Alchemy Gallery

- 🖼 157 Farringdon Road, EC1
- 🕾 0171 278 5666
- 🚌 Transport: Farringdon LU
- 🕐 Mon-Fri 9.30-18.00

Shows mainly photography, but with some contemporary art and ceramics.

Annely Juda Fine Art

- 🖼 23 Dering Street, W1
- 🕾 0171 629 7578
- 🚌 Transport: Bond Street LU
- 🕐 Mon-Fri 10.00-18.00, Sat 10.00-13.00

Top notch contemporary and modern art.

Anthony D'Offay Gallery

- 🖼 9, 21, 23 and 24 Dering Street, W1
- 🕾 0171 499 4100
- 🚌 Transport: Bond Street LU, Oxford Circus LU
- 🕐 Mon-Fri 10.00-17.30, Sat 10.00-13.00

Four exhibition spaces and a stellar list of artists make this London's largest commercial contemporary art gallery. D'Offay's constellation includes some of the biggest names in the business – from Carl Andre to Andy Warhol, via Gilbert & George, Roy Lichtenstein and Richard Long. New shows are staged every six weeks.

The Approach

- 🖼 1st Floor, 47 Approach Road, E2
- 🕾 0181 983 3878
- 🚌 Transport: Bethnal Green LU
- 🕐 Thurs-Fri 13.00-19.00, Sat-Sun 12.00-18.00

Located above The Approach Tavern, this gallery showcases young contemporary artists. Recent exhibitions have included a solo show by painter Peter Davies and a group show 'A-Z', curated by Matthew Higgs.

125

Anthony D'Offay Gallery

Artemis Group

🖼 *15 Duke Street, St James, SW1*
📞 *0171 930 8733*
🚌 *Transport: Green Park LU,*
   Piccadilly Circus LU
🕐 *Mon-Fri 9.30-17.30*

Old Masters and Impressionists.

Artmonsky Arts

🖼 *108a Boundary Road, NW8*
📞 *0171 604 3990*
🚌 *Transport: Swiss Cottage LU,*
   Kilburn Park LU, St. John's Wood LU,
   Maida Vale LU
🕐 *Tues-Sat 11.00-18.00*

Just a few doors along from the Saatchi Gallery, this spanking new gallery plans to show mainly contemporary art. A photography exhibition is scheduled for later in the year and ceramics are set to be a regularly featured. Bibliophiles and browsers should also enjoy the gallery's rare artist's monographs.

Association Gallery

🖼 *9-10 Domingo Street, EC1*
📞 *0171 608 1445*
🚌 *Transport: Old Street LU, Barbican LU*
🕐 *Mon-Fri 9.30-18.00, Sat 12.00-16.00*

A contemporary photography gallery, which holds some 20 exhibitions a year.

Austin/Desmond

🖼 *Pied Bull Yard,*
   68/69 Great Russell Street, WC1
📞 *0171 242 4443*
🚌 *Transport: Holborn LU, Tottenham Court*
   Road LU, Russell Square LU
🕐 *Mon-Fri 10.30-17.30, Sat 11.00-14.00*

Modern British paintings, ceramics and sculptures. Recent exhibitions have showcased the work of Keith Vaughan, Prunella Clough, David Jones and Wyndham Lewis.

Beaux Arts London

- *22 Cork Street, W1*
- *0171 437 5799*
- *Transport: Piccadilly Circus LU, Green Park LU*
- *Mon-Fri 10.00-18.00, Sat 10.00-14.00*

Best known for showing Modern British artists like Frink, Hepworth and names from the St Ives School, the gallery is beginning to diversify into contemporary and non-British art.

Belgrave Gallery

- *53 Englands Lane, NW3*
- *0171 722 5150*
- *Transport: Chalk Farm LU, Belsize Park LU*
- *Mon-Thurs 10.00-18.00, Fri 10.00-16.00, Sun 13.00-16.00*

Although somewhat off the beaten track for a commercial gallery, the Belgrave holds consistently interesting exhibitions of contemporary and C20th British art. A recent show included major names like Barbara Hepworth, Terry Frost and Victor Pasmore. Camomile, the patisserie a few doors down, serves delicious coffee and croissants to revive the hungry gallery-goer.

Bernard Jacobson

- *14a Clifford Street, W1*
- *0171 495 8575*
- *Transport: Piccadilly Circus LU, Green Park LU*
- *Mon-Fri 10.00-18.00, Sat 10.00-13.00*

Contemporary and Modern, with a particular focus on British art.

The Bloomsbury Workshop

- *12 Galen Place, off Bury Place, WC1*
- *0171 405 0632*
- *Transport: Holborn LU, Tottenham Court Road LU, Russell Square LU*
- *Mon-Fri 10.00-17.30*

Tucked away in a courtyard just by the British Museum, this tiny, charismatic art gallery and bookshop specialises in the art and literature of the Bloomsbury group. So, if you're not afraid of Virginia Woolf...

Boundary Gallery

- *98 Boundary Road, NW8*
- *0171 624 1126*
- *Transport: Swiss Cottage LU*
- *Wed-Sat 11.00-18.00 and by appointment*

Next door to the Saatchi Collection (p117), this gallery deals in figurative C20th art with specialisms in colourists and works by Anglo-Jewish artists.

Browse & Darby

- *19 Cork Street, W1*
- *0171 734 7984*
- *Transport: Piccadilly Circus LU, Green Park LU*
- *Mon-Fri 10.00-17.30*

Late C19th and early C20th English and French art, as well as contemporary paintings and sculpture.

The Cable Street Gallery

- *566 Cable Street, E1*
- *0171 790 1309*
- *Transport: Limehouse DLR*
- *Thurs-Sun 12.00-17.00*
- *Café*

Run by a collective of artists, this gallery aims to show a broad base of innovative contemporary art. New exhibitions are staged monthly and include installations, photography, painting and sculpture.

Camerawork

⌨ *121 Roman Road, E2*
☎ *0181 980 6256*
🚌 *Transport: Bethnal Green LU*
🕐 *Tues-Sat 13.00-18.00, Sun 12.00-18.00*
   (during exhibitions)
♿ *Wheelchair access*

Contemporary, predominantly lens based, art work.

Colnaghi

⌨ *15 Old Bond Street, W1*
☎ *0171 491 7408*
🚌 *Transport: Green Park LU,*
   Piccadilly Circus LU
🕐 *Mon-Fri 10.00-18.00*
   (Mon until 20.00), Sat 12.00-16.00

Old Master paintings and drawings.

Contemporary Applied Art

Contemporary Applied Art

⌨ *2 Percy Street, W1*
☎ *0171 436 2344*
🚌 *Transport: Goodge Street LU,*
   Tottenham Court Road LU
🕐 *Mon-Sat 10.30-17.30*

Deeply covetable jewellery, textiles, ceramics, furniture, metalwork and wood.

Cox and Company

⌨ *37 Duke Street, St James, SW1*
☎ *0171 930 1987*
🚌 *Transport: Green Park LU,*
   Piccadilly Circus LU
🕐 *Mon-Fri 10.00-17.30, Sat by appointment*

English landscape and sporting paintings plus C19th and C20th European oils and watercolours.

Crane Kalman

⌨ *178 Brompton Road, SW3*
☎ *0171 584 7566*
🚌 *Transport: Knightsbridge LU,*
   South Kensington LU
🕐 *Mon-Fri 10.00-18.00, Sat 10.00-16.00*

Specialists in post-war Modern British, international and contemporary art. Artists include Bomberg, Lowry, Mary Newcomb and Winifred Nicholson.

Dover Street Gallery & Arthur Tooth & Sons

⌨ *13 Dover Street, W1*
☎ *0171 409 1540*
🚌 *Transport: Green Park LU,*
   Piccadilly Circus LU
🕐 *Mon-Fri 10.00-18.00, Sat 11.30-16.00*

One of the only galleries in London to specialise in the art of the Viennese Secession (carrying work by Gustav Klimt and Egon Schiele among others), this establishment also deals in Italian and French Old Masters from the C16th-C19th.

The Eagle Gallery

- 159 Farringdon Road, EC1
- 0171 833 2674
- Transport: Farringdon LU
- Thur-Fri 11.00-18.00,
  Sat-Sun 11.00-16.00 and by appointment

Mainly conceptual and abstract art on show here, although the gallery also publishes limited edition artists' books.

Entwistle Gallery

- 6 Cork Street, W1
- 0171 734 6440
- Transport: Piccadilly Circus LU,
  Green Park LU
- Mon-Fri 10.00-17.50, Sat 11.00-16.30

Contemporary, tribal and C19th and C20th art.

Fine Art Society

- 148 New Bond Street, W1
- 0171 629 5116
- Transport: Green Park LU,
  Bond Street LU
- Mon-Fri 9.30-17.30, Sat 10.00-13.00

If you're trawling up Bond Street having done the rounds of Cork Street, keep some time and energy in reserve for this superb gallery. Always a pleasure to visit, the Society stocks a carefully edited selection of British art from 1840-1960.

Flowers East

- 199-205 and 282 Richmond Road, E8
- 0181 985 3333
- Transport: Bethnal Green LU (then bus)
- Tues-Sun 10.00-18.00   .

Contemporary art with a bias towards the figurative and with a strong graphics element. The gallery's artists include Peter Howson, Nicola Hicks and Terry Frost.

Writing Cabinet from The Fine Art Society

Frith Street Gallery

- 60 Frith Street, W1
- 0171 494 1550
- Transport: Tottenham Court Road LU
- Tues-Fri 10.00-18.00, Sat 11.00-16.00

Contemporary art by both British and international artists.

Frost & Reed

- 2-4 King Street, St James, SW1
- 0171 839 4645
- Transport: Green Park LU,
  Piccadilly Circus LU
- Mon-Fri 9.00-17.30

British, French and sporting paintings from the C19th and C20th.

GALLERIES -COMMERCIAL

129

Galerie Besson

⊡ *15 Royal Arcade, 28 Old Bond Street, W1*
🕿 *0171 491 1706*
🚌 *Transport: Green Park LU,*
    Piccadilly Circus LU
🕐 *Tues-Fri 10.00-17.30*
    (Mon by appointment only 13.00-17.30)

Ceramics gallery showing works by C20th masters like Lucie Rie, Hans Coper and Bernard Leech as well as more contemporary names like Jim Malone.

Gasworks

⊡ *155 Vauxhall Street, SE11*
🕿 *0171 735 3445*
🚌 *Transport: Oval LU*
🕐 *Fri-Sun 12.00-18.00 (or by appointment)*
♿ *Wheelchair Access*

A small artist-led gallery, Gasworks shows works by young British and International artists.

Gimpel Fils

⊡ *30 Davies Street, W1*
🕿 *0171 493 2488*
🚌 *Transport: Bond Street LU*
🕐 *Mon-Fri 10.00-17.30, Sat 10.00-13.00*

Long-established gallery showing modern and contemporary art.

Portrait of a Moor by Bartholomäus Maton from Johnny van Haeften Gallery

Interim Art

🖃 21 Beck Road, E8
☎ 0171 254 9607
🚌 Transport: Bethnal Green LU (then bus)
🕐 Fri and Sat 11.00-18.00
    and by appointment

Contemporary British art – and how. The gallery represents about 15 YBA's including Mark Francis and recent Turner Prize winner Gillian Wearing.

Jason & Rhodes

🖃 4 New Burlington Place, W1
☎ 0171 434 1768
🚌 Transport: Piccadilly Circus LU
🕐 Mon-Fri 10.30-18.00, Sat 10.30-13.00

Contemporary painting, photography and sculpture.

Jay Jopling/White Cube

🖃 2nd Floor, 44 Duke Street St James, W1
☎ 0171 930 5373
🚌 Transport: Green Park LU
🕐 Fri and Sat 12.00-18.00
    and by appointment

So cutting edge it hurts, White Cube is the ne plus ultra of commercial galleries dealing in contemporary art. Perhaps most famous for representing Damien Hirst, Jopling also exhibits a range of young European and British artists. All works on display are specially commissioned for the gallery.

Jill George Gallery

🖃 38 Lexington Street, W1
☎ 0171 439 7319
🚌 Transport: Tottenham Court Road LU
🕐 Mon-Fri 10.00-18.00, Sat 11.00-16.00

Contemporary British paintings, drawings, watercolours and prints.

Johnny van Haeften Gallery

🖃 13 Duke Street, St James SW1
☎ 0171 930 3062
🚌 Transport: Green Park LU,
    Piccadilly Circus LU
🕐 Mon-Fri 10.00-18.00,
    Sat-Sun by appointment

The gallery's recent 20th Anniversary winter exhibition included works by Brueghel and de Hooch.

Lamont Gallery

🖃 67 Roman Road, E8
☎ 9181 981 6332
🚌 Transport: Bethnal Green LU
🕐 Tues-Sat 11.00-18.00

Housed in a converted pub, the Lamont Gallery was the first commercial gallery to open in East London. Thirteen years later the gallery is thriving and remains as dedicated as ever to making contemporary art accessible to the public. Although sculpture is occasionally on view, representational painting is the thing to see here and gallery artists include Graham Crowley, Robin Mason and Sonia Lawson.

London Electronic Arts

🖃 LUX Centre, 2-4 Hoxton Square, N1
☎ 0171 684 2785
🚌 Transport: Old Street LU
🕐 Wed-Fri 12.00-19.00, Sat-Sun 12.00-18.00
🍴 Cafe/bar
♿ Wheelchair Access

Launched in October 1997, LEA specialises in film, video and computer-based artworks. To complement its innovative exhibition programme, the gallery's four huge windows are used for night time projections by artists like Gary Hume and Mat Collishaw – ideal for after hours gallery goers. Located in ultra hip Hoxton Square, the LUX Centre is also home to the cinema of the same name.

GALLERIES -COMMERCIAL

131

A Metre of Meadow by Mark Dion at London Projects

The Lefevre Gallery (Alex Reid & Lefevre Ltd)

🖻 *30 Bruton Street, W1*
🕾 *0171 493 2107*
🚌 *Transport: Green Park LU, Bond Street LU*
🕒 *Mon-Fri 10.00-17.00*

This gallery shows works by Impressionists and Post-Impressionists, but will shortly have a whole floor devoted to contemporary art as well.

Lisson Gallery

🖻 *67 Lisson Street, NW1*
🕾 *0171 724 2739*
🚌 *Transport: Marylebone LU, Edgware Road LU*
🕒 *Mon-Fri 10.00-18.00, Sat 10.00-17.00*

Contemporary British art. Recent single artist shows have included Mat Collishaw and Anish Kapoor.

London Projects

🖻 *47 Frith Street, W1*
🕾 *0171 734 1723*
🚌 *Transport: Tottenham Court Road LU*
🕒 *Fri and Sat 10.00-18.00, Mon-Thurs by appointment only*

Mark Dion, Uta Barth and Alexis Rockman are among the contemporary international artists who have exhibited at this gallery.

Lotta Hammer

🖻 *51a Cleveland Street, W1*
🕾 *0171 636 2221*
🚌 *Transport: Goodge Street LU*
🕒 *Tues-Fri 11.00-18.00, Sat 12.00-16.00*

Up-and-coming artists, mainly British. Paintings and installations.

The Maas Gallery

🖃 *15a Clifford Street, W1*
🕾 *0171 734 2302*
🚌 *Transport: Piccadilly Circus LU,*
  Green Park LU
🕔 *Mon-Fri 10.00-17.30*

Victorian and Pre-Raphaelite art. 'Antiques Roadshow' viewers will recognise proprietor Rupert Maas as one of the art experts on the programme.

Marlborough Fine Art

🖃 *6 Albemarle Street, W1*
🕾 *0171 629 5161*
🚌 *Transport: Green Park LU*
🕔 *Mon-Fri 10.00-17.30, Sat 10.00-12.30*

Another big name on the contemporary art scene. Marlborough's impressive stable includes Frank Auerbach and Paula Rego, and the gallery also sells graphics by modern masters like Picasso.

The Mayor Gallery

🖃 *22a Cork Street, W1*
🕾 *0171 734 3558*
🚌 *Transport: Piccadilly Circus LU,*
  Green Park LU
🕔 *Mon-Fri 10.00-17.30, Sat 10.00-13.00*

Specialists in Dada and Surrealist art, the gallery also shows pop art and works by British artists.

New End Gallery

🖃 *25 Carnegie House,*
  New End/Well Road, NW3
🕾 *0171 431 4664*
🚌 *Transport: Hampstead LU*
🕔 *Wed-Sun 14.00-18.00 or by appointment*

Hidden away in deepest Hampstead, this diminutive gallery shows predominantly issue based work by both young and established artists. Past exhibitions have featured Vivien Henry and Michael Peel.

The Piccadilly Gallery

🖃 *43 Dover Street, W1*
🕾 *0171 629 2875*
🚌 *Transport: Piccadilly Circus LU,*
  Green Park LU
🕔 *Mon-Fri 10.00-17.30, Sat 10.30-13.00*

The gallery shows C20th British figurative artists such as Royal Academician Anthony Green as well as dealing in Art Nouveau and the Belgian Symbolists.

Purdy Hicks Gallery

🖃 *65 Hopton Street, SE1*
🕾 *0171 401 9229*
🚌 *Transport: Blackfriars LU*
🕔 *Mon, Tues, Thur, Fri 10.00-17.30,*
  Wed 10.00-19.00, Sat 10.00-14.00

Estelle Thompson and Arturo di Stefano are among the 14 contemporary artists represented by this Southwark-based gallery. Eight to ten one-person shows are held a year, usually with a concurrent exhibition in the downstairs gallery.

Rebecca Hossack Gallery

🖃 *35 Windmill Street, W1*
🕾 *0171 436 4899*
🚌 *Transport: Goodge Street LU*
🕔 *Mon-Sat 10.00-18.00*

Specialists in Aboriginal art and contemporary European art.

Redfern Gallery

🖃 *20 Cork Street, W1*
🕾 *0171 734 1732*
🚌 *Transport: Piccadilly Circus LU,*
  Green Park LU
🕔 *Mon-Fri 10.00-17.30, Sat 10.00-13.00*

Contemporary and modern paintings, drawings and prints. Gallery artists include Patrick Procktor, Paul Feiler and Annabel Gault.

GALLERIES -COMMERCIAL

Richard Salmon

- Studios 3 and 4,
  59 South Edwardes Square, W8
- 0171 602 9494
- Transport: High Street Kensington LU
- Tues-Sat 10.00-18.00

An eclectic selection of contemporary art in a variety of media, including video and photography.

Rocket Gallery

- 13 Old Burlington Street, W1
- 0171 434 3043
- Transport: Piccadilly Circus LU, Green Park LU
- Tues-Sat 10.00-18.00

Rocket works with international artists, specialising in abstract and minimalist work, as well exhibiting work by photographers such as Martin Parr. Part of the Rocket Press, the gallery also stocks limited edition artists' books.

Sadie Coles HQ

- 35 Heddon Street, W1
- 0171 434 2227
- Transport: Piccadilly Circus LU, Oxford Circus LU
- Tues-Sat 10.00-18.00

This gallery shows young contemporary art – like the work of 'Sensation' sculptor Sarah Lucas. A relative newcomer to the scene (it opened in April 1997), the HQ has exciting plans for the future, including off-site exhibitions in collaboration with the Chapman brothers.

The Special Photographers Company

- 21 Kensington Park Road, W11
- 0171 221 3489
- Transport: Ladbroke Grove LU, Notting Hill Gate LU, Holland Park LU
- Mon-Fri 10.00-18.00, Sat 11.00-17.00

Fine art photography with a bias towards personal rather than commercial work.

Photograph by Etienne Clement at The Special Photographers Gallery

Spink & Son Ltd

- 5, 6 and 7 King Street, St James, SW1
- 0171 930 7888
- Transport: Piccadilly Circus LU, Green Park LU
- Mon-Fri 9.00-17.30

Founded in 1666, this is one of the oldest art dealers in the world. The company's 14 departments cover a huge spectrum of art including Indian and Oriental art, textiles, English furniture and paintings from C17th to present day, as well as collectables such as stamps, coins and medals.

Standpoint Gallery

- 45 Coronet Street, N1
- 0171 739 4921
- Transport: Old Street LU
- Wed-Sun 12.00-18.00 (telephone for exhibition dates)

Work by contemporary artists working in a variety of media, including ceramics, printmaking and bookbinding as well as painting and photography. A programme of gallery talks accompanies each exhibition.

Stephen Friedman Gallery

- 25-28 Old Burlington Street, W1
- 0171 794 1434
- Transport: Piccadilly Circus LU, Green Park LU
- Tues-Fri 10.00-18.00, Sat 11.00-17.00

Contemporary international art. Look out for the funky urban garden at the rear of the gallery.

Stoppenbach & Delestre

- 25 Cork Street, W1
- 0171 734 3534
- Transport: Piccadilly Circus LU, Green Park LU
- Mon-Fri 10.00-17.30, Sat 10.00-13.00

French C19th & C20th art, including works by the Barbizon school, can be found at this gallery.

Theo Waddington Fine Art

- 5a Cork Street, W1
- 0171 494 1584
- Transport: Piccadilly Circus LU, Green Park LU
- Tues-Fri 11.00-18.00, Sat 11.00-17.00

Theo Waddington shows a diverse range of art – his stable of artists includes David Inshaw and Joe Tilson but you're just as likely to see works by Irish expressionist J.B. Yeats or the American painter Milton Avery or modern classics by Matisse, Dufy and Laurens.

Timothy Taylor Gallery

- 1 Bruton Place, W1
- 0171 409 3344
- Transport: Bond Street LU, Green Park LU
- Mon-Fri 10.00-18.00, Sat 11.00-14.00

Modern and contemporary art – with the emphasis on abstract painting. Sean Scully and Miquel Barcelo are both represented by the gallery.

30 Underwood Street Gallery

- 30-34 Underwood Street, N1
- 0171 336 0884
- Transport: Old Street LU, Angel LU
- Fri-Sun 13.00-18.00 or by appointment

With an international reputation for its innovative programme of visual and live arts, the gallery shows contemporary art with a capital C.

GALLERIES -COMMERCIAL

135

Victoria Miro

⊡ 21 Cork Street, W1
☏ 0171 734 5082
🚌 Transport: Piccadilly Circus LU,
    Green Park LU
🕒 Mon-Fri 10.00-17.30, Sat 11.00-13.00

Hip, happening, and contemporary.

Waddington Galleries

⊡ 11, 12 and 34 Cork Street, W1
☏ 0171 437 8611
🚌 Transport: Green Park LU, Piccadilly LU
🕒 Mon-Fri 10.00-17.30, Sat 10.00-13.00

Established in the 60's, Waddingtons is
still swinging and a regular haunt for
collectors and scruffy art students alike.
Expect to see blue chip modern and classy
contemporary art at this three gallery Cork
Street emporium. Sculptor Barry Flanagan
and YBA's Ian Davenport and Fiona Rae
are among the contemporary artists
represented.

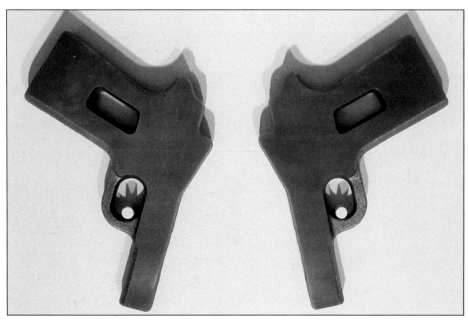

Embryo Firearms, Cornelia Parker, Frith Street Gallery

APPENDIX

Exhibition and Heritage Venues

Age Exchange Reminiscence Centre
11 Blackheath Village
London
SE3 9LA
0181 318 9105

This voluntary organisation arranges meetings so that young people can understand the past by listening to the reminiscences of the old. The organisation also runs a small museum and shop.

Battersea Arts Centre
Old Town Hall
Lavender Hill
London
SW11 5TF
0171 223 2223
0171 223 6557

The BAC gallery hosts regular exhibitions.

Business Design Centre
52 Upper Street
Islington Green
London
N1 0QH
0171 359 3535

This is the venue for the Contemporary Arts Fair which is held every January, as well as other events around the calender.

Canada House Gallery
Trafalgar Square
London
SW1Y 5BJ
0171 258 6600

Canada House hosts regular exhibitions and has only recently re-opened after a period of refurbishment.

London Arts Cafe
108 Boundaries Road
SW12 8HQ
0181 767 7148 (evenings)

The LAC is a forum for viewing, expressing and discovering all forms of urban art, Its mission is to highlight urban artistic developments in the capital, in the United Kingdom and all over the world. Launched in 1996, the LAC (which is a charitable organisation) provides a unique platform for the art of cities and organises a stimulating programme of exhibits and special events at venues around the capital. well worth seeking out.

The Mall Galleries
The Mall
London
SW1
0171 930 6844

The Mall Galleries represent the work of nine art societies as well as being used by other artists. Exhibitions change regularly so it's advisable to phone in advance before visiting.

Museum of Installation
175 Deptford High Street
London SE8
0181 692 8778

This is a venue for contemporary installation art, rather than a museum. Exhibitions change regularly so it's a good idea to ring in advance.

Royal College of Art Gallery

Kensington Gore
London
SW7 2EU
0171 590 4444

The Royal College stages its degree show between May and July, but also plays host to regular touring shows. Opening times are 10am-8pm weekdays, and 10am-6pm at weekends – phone to check what's showing.

Southside House

Wimbledon Common
London
SW19 4RJ
0181 946 7643

Privately owned, this historic house is open to the public between January and June on Tuesday, Thursday and Saturday afternoons (2pm-5pm). Visits are by guided tour only.

Thames Barrier Visitors Centre

Unity Way
Woolwich
London
SE18 5NJ
0181 854 1373
Open: Sat–Sun 10.30am-4.30pm, Mon–Fri 10am–4.00pm
Admission Charge: £3.40 (Adults), £2.40 (Children/OAP's), £7.50 (Families)

The Visitor Centre gives you a great view of the barrier and includes an audio/visual show and exhibition in the price.

Archives & Libraries

Ashmole Archive

Dept of Classics
King's College London
Strand
London
WC2R 2LS
0171 873 2343

The Ashmole is a photographic archive of ancient Greek sculpture, which is open to view by appointment only.

Book Trust

Book House
45 East Hill
London
SW18 2QZ
0181 516 2977

An independent charity founded to promote reading. The Book Trust keeps a collection of children's books, as well as a database of all books in print.

British Library

96 Euston Road
London
NW1 2DB
0171 412 7222
http://www.bl.uk/

The British Library Galleries are already mentioned within this book, but the library has many other services and events including lectures, just about the largest collection of books in the world, a bookshop and educational services.

British Olympic Library

1 Wandsworth Plain
London
SW18 1EH
0181 871 2677

This library contains everything to do with the Olympics and British Olympians. Phone in advance for an appointment before visiting.

Fawcett Library

London Guildhall University
Old Castle Street
London
E1 7NT
0171 320 1189
www.lgu.ac.uk/phil/fawcett.htm

This archive of women's literature and reference material has just received over £4 million of Lottery money to help restore and maintain its valuable resources.

Hammersmith and Fulham Archives and Local History Centre

The Lilla Huset
191 Talgarth Road
London
W6 8BJ
0181 741 5159

Phone in advance to make an appointment.

Lambeth Palace Library

Lambeth Palace Road
London
SE1 7JU
0171 928 6222
Open: Monday–Friday 10am–5pm

This library specialises in church history, history and family history (genealogy).

Marx Memorial Library

37a Clerkenwell Green
London
EC1R 0DU
0171 253 1485

Currently closed for refurbishment, but will re-open in January 1999.

National Monuments Record

55 Blandford Street
London
W1H 3AF
0171 208 8200
Open: Tues-Fri 10am-5pm

The National Monuments Record holds a wonderful photographic collection of London's streets and buildings.

National Sound Archive

(part of The British Library)
96 Euston Road
London
NW1 2DB
0171 589 6603
Open: Mon–Fri 9.30-6pm, Sat 9.30–5pm

This extensive collection of music, wildlife sounds and oral recordings is open to academics by appointment.

Professional Bodies

British Tourist Authority
Head Office
Thames Tower
Black's Road
London
W6 9EL
0181 846 9000

Contemporary Art Society
17 Bloomsbury Square
London
WC1A 2LP
0171 831 7311

This charity promotes contemporary art and raises funds for the collection of some of the country's most challenging work.

English Heritage
Fortress House
Savile Row
London
W1X 1AB
0171 973 3000

English Heritage owns historic houses throughout the country. If you want to find out more, phone and ask for an information pack.

Museums and Galleries Commission
16 Queen Anne's Gate
London
SW1H 9AA
0171 233 4200

This organisation acts as an advocate for museums and galleries and promotes the highest standards in museum and gallery practice.

Museums and Galleries Disability Association (MAGDA)
c/o William Kirby
11 Eastgate Street
Winchester
Hampshire
SO23 8EB
01962 854 003

This association is concerned with promoting equal access to museums and galleries for disabled people.

The National Art Collections Fund
7 Cromwell Place
London
SW7 2JN
0171 225 4800

Becoming a member of the NACF costs £25 per year and gives free entry to many museums and galleries as well as discounts on many special exhibitions, and a free magazine. Your money contributes funds for the purchase of works of art for Britain's museums and galleries.

The National Trust
Membership Department
PO Box 39
Bromley
Kent
BR1 3XL
0181 315 1111

Founded in 1895 this independent heritage charity today protects some 350 gardens and houses, over 550 miles of coastline and 600,000 acres of countryside across England, Wales and Northern Ireland.

London Degree Shows

Degree and foundation shows are held by art colleges and universities in London during the summer months from May to August. They are a great opportunity to view the latest in art and craft, and if you attend on the opening day you can mingle with young and very attractive art students, view their creations and enjoy wine and cheese nibbles. Contact details for the various London art institutions are listed below. For current information about degree shows throughout the country the Candid Arts Trust have established a web site (**DegreeShow.net**)

Byam Shaw School of Art

2 Elthorne Road
Archway
London
N19 4AG
Tel: 0171 281 4111
Contact name: Thelma Wimyard

The degree show is normally held at the end of June. For further information phone the above number.

Camberwell College of Arts

Peckham Road
London
SE5 8UF

Wilsons Road
London
SE5 8LU

Tel: 0171 514 6301
Contact: Silvia Butcher

The degree/MA and foundation shows are held during May and June on both sites. Contact the above number for details.

Central Saint Martins College of Art and Design

Southampton Row
London WC1
Subjects: Ceramics, Jewellery, Product Design, Textile Design, Theatre Design, Advanced Stained Glass, Fashion Shows
June-July

107-109 Charing Cross Road
London WC2
Subjects: Fashion, Fine Art, Photography
June-July

27-29 Long Acre
London WC2
Subject: Graphic Design
June-July

Saffron House
Back Hill
London EC1
and
13-15 Eagle Court
St John's Lane EC1
Subject: Foundation Show
June

For further information contact Edward Goldswain on 0171 514 7022.

Chelsea College of Art & Design

Bagleys Lane and Hugo Road
London, SW6
Subject: Foundation/NDD, Fine Art
June (Foundation), August (Fine Art)

Manresa Road
London, SW3
Subject: Design
June

For further information contact the central office on 0171 514 7751.

Cordwainers College
182 Mare Street
London
E8 3RE
0181 985 0273
(ask for the marketing department)

Shows are held in June and July both on the college site and at an external location. In 1998 the external show was held at the Barbican Centre.

Goldsmiths College
New Cross
London
SE14 6NW
0171 919 7282 (the Visual Arts Department)

Shows are held from the end of May. Phone the visual arts department for more information.

Kingston University
53-7 High Street
Kingston upon Thames
KT1 1LQ
0181 547 7066
Contact name: Diana Lawson

The university's degree show includes the work of fashion designers, photographers, graphic artists and students of fine art. For further details contact Diana Lawson at the above number.

London College of Fashion
Most of the degree shows are by invitation only. For further details contact Sarah Wilshaw 0171 514 7565

London College of Printing
All the various sites and subjects are listed below. For further information contact Simon Pamplin on 0171 514 6509.

Graphic Design Studios
Elephant and Castle
London SE1
Subjects: Graphic and Media Design
June

Eckersley Gallery and Refectory
Elephant and Castle
London SE1
Subjects: Graphic Design, Typography, Creative Media
June, July (Creative Media)

Sub-basement and Foyer
Saffron House
Black Hill
Clerkenwell EC1
Subjects: Media Foundation, Photography and Photojournalism
June

The National Film Theatre
South Bank
London SE1
Subjects: Film and Video
July

3rd Floor
65 Davies Street
London W1
Subject: Retail Design
June

Atrium Gallery
Whitleys
Queensway
London W2
Subject: Printmaking Techniques
June

London Guildhall University

133 Whitechapel High Street
London
E1 7QA
0171 320 1000

The university hosts its degree show in June each year and includes disciplines like fine art, design, restoration and jewellery making.

Middlesex University

White Hart Lane
London
N17 8HR
0181 362 6107
Contact name: Nicola Barker

Middlesex University holds its degree show in June and displays work from many disciplines from printed textiles to jewellery design to fine art. Phone Nicola Baker at the above number for full details.

Roehampton Institute London

(An Institute of Surrey University)
Roehampton Lane
London
SW15 5PU
0181 392 3653
Contact name: Caroline Styles

The institute has a show in June which includes calligraphy and bookbinding, painting, ceramics, photography, mosaics and print making. For further information contact the above number.

Royal College of Art

The Royal College hosts its degree show on two sites between June and July. The fine and applied art, design, architecture and graphics are held at the Kensington Gore address, while sculpture is exhibited at the Howie Street site.

Kensington Gore
SW7 2EU
0171 590 4444

The Sculpture School
15-25 Howie Street
Battersea
SW11 4AS

Contact the main office for details.

The Slade School of Art

University College London
Gower Street
WC1E 6BT
0171 504 2313
Contact: Rebecca Tilley

The Slade School shows both under graduate and post graduate shows in May and June. The disciplines covered include fine art, sculpture and theatre design.

University of East London

Greengate House
Greengate Road
London
E13 0BG
0181 849 3691

The UEL holds degree shows throughout June including subjects such as fine art, textile design and photography.

Wimbledon School of Art

Main Building
Merton Hall Road
Wimbledon
SW19 3QA
0181 408 5000

This school holds its degree and diploma shows in June and July and includes sculpture, printmaking, fine art and theatre design. For more information contact the above number.

INDEX

INDEX

INDEX

Photography Credits

p.3 People in Tate Gallery © Liam Bailey / p.6 Italian Cast Courts © The Victoria and Albert Museum, Tiles from Cinderella © William Morris Gallery, Couch designed by Dali © The Museum of the Moving Image/ p.7 The Wellington Museum at Dusk courtesy of Apsley House press office / p.10 The Dying Lioness © The British Museum / p.12 Sutton Hoo buckle © The British Museum / p.14 Winston Churchill on the Phone courtesy of The Cabinet War Rooms / p.16 The Design Museum © Jefferson Smith / p.18 The Florence Nightingale Museum Courtesy of the Florence Nightingale Museum / p.19 The Golden Hinde © Golden Hinde Ltd / p.20 The Grand Temple vestibule ceiling © Freemason's Hall London / p.23 Imperial War Museum © Imperial War Museum / p.27 The London Transport Museum © London Transport Museum / p.29 Roman Wall Painting © Museum of London / p.30 The Hand of Mithras © Museum of London / p.31 False Maria from Fritz Lang's Metropolis © The Museum of the Moving Image / p.35 The Herb Garret © The Old Operating Theatre / p.37 Mummy Portrait © The Petrie Museum / p.39 Shakespeare's Globe Theatre © Richard Kalina / p.40 The Soane's Museum © Martin Charles / p.41 Costume Workshops at the Theatre Museum © Graham Brandon / p.42 Towers Bridge: View from the east Walkway © Tower Bridge / p.44 Chief Yeoman Warder by Yves Salmon, © Crown Copyright HRP / p.45 Twinings in the Strand © Twinings / p.47 Science for Life, The Welcome Trust, © The Welcome Trust / p.48 Dolls' House at Bethnal Green Museum of Childhood © Trustees of the Victoria and Albert Museum / p.49 The Regency Room, The Geffrye Museum © The Geffrye Museum / p.50 A Mask Making Workshop, The Ragged School Museum © The Ragged School Museum Trust / p.52 The Little Chamber, Sutton House © The National Trust / p.53 History of Godfrey of Boloyne © William Morris Gallery / p.54 Arsenal Football Club Museum © Arsenal Football Club Museum / p.56 Freud's psychoanalytic couch © The Freud Museum / p.57 The Guitar Player by Vermeer from The Iveagh Bequest © English Heritage / p.58 The Torah Scrolls by Frederick Kandler © The Jewish Museum London / p.60 The Royal Airforce Museum © The RAF Museum / p.64 The Cutty Sark courtesy of The National Maritime Museum / p.65 Contemporary Fan © The Fan Museum / p.66 The Horniman Museum courtesy of the Horniman Museum / p.68 Captain Horatio Nelson by Jean Francis Rigaud © The National Maritme Museum / p.69 Old Royal Observatory © National Maritime Museum Greenwich / p.70 The Tulip Staircase in the Queen's House © National Maritime Museum / p.71 Anne Cecil © Ranger's House / p.73 Racket Makers Workshop © Wimbledon Lawn Tennis Museum / p.75 Chiswick House © English Heritage / p.77 The Arab Hall © Leighton House Museum / p.78 The London Toy and Model Museum © The London Toy and Model Museum / p.80 Mortuary Sword © National Army Museum / p.82 The Central Hall © The Natural History Museum / p.84 Museum of Instruments © The Royal College of Music / p.85 Exploration of Space © The Science Museum / p.87 Flight Exhibition © The Science Museum / p.88 The Silver Galleries © The Victoria and Albert Museum / p.89 Italian Cast Courts © The Victoria and Albert Museum / p.91 The William Morris Society courtesy of the William Morris Society / p.97 Hampton Court Palace by Howard Sayer © Crown Copyright, HRP / p.100 Gino Severini, Le Boulevard © ADAGP, Paris and DACS, L.Walpole © Crafts Council/ p.104 The Institute of Contemporary Arts by David Tucker © The ICA / p.105 The Ambassadors by Hans Holbein © The National Gallery / p.107 People in the National Gallery © The National Gallery / p.109 The Photographers' Gallery © The Photographers' Gallery / p.110 The Royal Academy of Arts by Phil Sayer © Royal Academy of Arts / p.111 The Tate Gallery by Marcus Leith © The Tate Gallery p.112 Captain Thomas Coram by William Hogarth © The Thomas Coram Foundation / p.113 Lady Hamilton courtesy of The Wallace Collection / p.114 Matt's Gallery courtesy of Matt's Gallery / p.115 The Sabbath Rest by Samuel Hirszenberg © Ben Uri Art Society / p.116 Glass bowl by Ray Flavell courtesy of The Arts Council / p.117 Young British Artists VI courtesy of The Saatchi Collection London / p.119 Dulwich Picture Gallery courtesy of the Dulwich Picture Gallery / p.120 South Gallery the Serpentine Gallery by Richard Bryant/Arcaid copyright artworks / p.121 Orleans House Gallery © Orleans House Gallery / p.125 Family Group by John Wonnacott courtesy of Agnew's (Old Bond Street) / p.126 Once I Saw a Bird by Kiki Smith courtesy of Anthony d'Offay / p.128 Contemporary Applied Art courtesy of Contemporary Applied Art / p.129 Writing Cabinet (1902-3) courtesy of The Fine Art Society / p.130 Portrait of a Moor by Bartholomaus Maton courtesy of Johnny Van Haeften Ltd / p.132 A Metre of Meadow by Mark Dion courtesy of London Projects / p.134 The Special Photographers Company © Etienne Clement / p.136 Embryo Firearms by Cornelia Parker courtesy of Frith Street Gallery.

METRO PUBLICATIONS

Bargain Hunters' London
Author: Andrew Kershman
£5.99, 144pp, 40 b/w photos, 12 Maps.
ISBN 0-9522914-2-8
Bargain Hunters' London reviews over 500 bargain outlets. Within its pages you can find just about any item (new or used), as well as tips about bartering and maps to help plan bargain days out in the capital. Bargain Hunters' features designer sales, electrical wholesalers, cheap street fashion, auctions, charity shops and much more.

Gay London
Author: Graham Parker
£5.99, 144pp, 40 b/w photos, 4 Maps,
ISBN 0-9522914-6-0
Gay London includes reviews of all the social clubs, political organisations, health services, restaurants and night clubs to help gay men enjoy the Capital. The book is an essential reference manual for those wishing to explore the capital's gay scene, and the most up to date book of its kind.

Food Lovers' London
Author: Jenny Linford
£5.99, 144pp, 40 b/w photos.
ISBN 0-9522914-5-2
Food Lovers' London contains all the information a London foodie needs to start cooking any of the thirteen nationalities of cuisine featured. Each cuisine has a glossary of ingredients and reviews of all the best food shops and eating places, as well as a brief history of the people and culture that gave rise to the food.

The London Market Guide
Author: Andrew Kershman
£3.99, 80pp, 60 b/w photos, 80 Maps.
ISBN 0-9522914-0-1
The London Market Guide contains all the essential information to explore London's 70 street markets with maps, photos, travel information, consumer tips, over 90 cafes and full contact details for those wanting to get a stall. The more popular markets like Portobello and Camden receive special attention, with details about the best days to visit if you want to avoid the crowds, and detailed maps.

Veggie London
Author: Craig John Wilson
£5.99, 112pp, 30 b/w photos.
ISBN 0-9522914-1-X
Craig Wilson has reviewed over 120 of the capital's vegetarian restaurants, in an attempt to escape from the veggie burger and find the best in vegetarian cuisine. Many of the restaurants listed also serve meat (for those who don't mind socialising with carnivores). The book also includes wholefood stores, vegetarian caterers, social and pressure groups.

Taste of London
Author: Jenny Linford
£6.99, 144pp, 55 b/w photos.
ISBN 0-9522914-7-9
Jenny Linford has chosen over eighty recipes inspired by the ingredients on offer in London's cosmopolitan markets and shops. If you've strolled around Chinatown or Brixton Market but never quite known what ingredients to buy or then this book is for you.